BREAKING THE BIAS OF ENGLISH

BREAKING THE BIAS OF ENGLISH

How English Disempowers Women and How to Fix It In Six Words

Vivian R. Probst

With Anne Wondra

Introducing WEnglish for WEquality™

PRIMIX
PUBLISHING
THE WRITE CHOICE

Primix Publishing
485c US Highway 1 South
Suite 100
Iselin, NJ 08830
www.primixpublishing.com
Phone: 1-800-538-5788

Published by Primix Publishing: 09/27/2024

ISBN: 979-8-89194-290-5(sc)
ISBN: 979-8-89194-291-2(e)

Library of Congress Control Number: 2024916418

This Book is Dedicated to

Generations of women whose work has gone uncredited, whose discoveries are considered of merit, yet the women themselves remain invisible.

Women whose contributions were credited to men
because they were deemed inconsequential, even though
they worked tirelessly with little compensation.

Women who raised families and overcame obstacles behind the scenes, endured the label of being considered "less than" by men while passionately engaging in brilliant work that went unseen.

To all these women who persevered through incredible challenges,

I owe great gratitude. Their courage laid the
underpinnings of my life's work with words—

Driving me into the depths of our world's most common language
to uncover the essence of a man's English and the miracle of
breaking that code so that we can all partake equally…

In a language that is neutralized with one word, giving
us some words of our own and thereby balancing a "he"
language into a "WE" language as it should be!

***

And to Anne Wondra, who has traveled with me on my writing pilgrimages for over a decade—a true and wise companion and the wind beneath my wings on yet another adventure.

"Thus the task is *not* to see what no one has yet seen but to think what nobody yet has thought about that which everybody sees."
– Arthur Schopenhauer, *Notable Pessimist*

"The hardest thing about writing is telling the truth." –
Sue Monk Kidd, *Dance of the Dissident Daughter*

Other works by Vivian Probst

Short Story Fiction:
The Little Black Book for BLUE People (Award winner)
The TimeMaker's Shop
A Dog Named goD

Fiction
Death by Roses (Award winner)

The Avery Victoria Spencer Fables, Books One to Four

Book One:
English: The Woman Who Forgot Who She Was
WEnglish for Equality: Tha Womun Who Forgot Who Shi Was

Book Two:
English: The Woman Who Fell Out of Fear
WEnglish for WEquality: Tha Womun Who Fell Out of Fear

Book Three:
English: The Woman Who Found Her Fire
WEnglish for WEquality: Tha Womun Who Found Hir Fire

Book Four:
English: The Woman Who Forgave Herself
WEnglish for Equality: Tha Womun Who Forgave Hirself

Non-fiction Memoir
I Was a Yo-Yo Wife…Until I Learned THIS!

Other Non-fiction:
Breaking The Bias of English

BREAKING THE BIAS OF ENGLISH:

How English Disempowers Women And How
To Fix It in **ONLY SIX WORDS**

Contents

Introduction and Glossary

IMPORTANT:

To read this book as intended, it is necessary to establish the definitions of certain words that are used throughout.

NOTE: I am a linguist, not a sexologist. Therefore, I beg tolerance as I may have selected words with different connotations for the more gender-focused among us. My objective is to equalize ENGLISH to include women.

For ease of reading, I have used regular English until each of the six words is explained.

Glossary of Terms
According to Merriam-Webster's Dictionary, these terms are defined as follows:

Adult: Fully developed and mature

Bias: An unreasoned and unfair distortion of judgment in favor of or against a person or thing

Equal: Alike in quality, nature, or status

Equality: The quality or state of being equal

Female: An individual of the sex that is typically capable of bearing young or producing eggs

Gender: Among those who study gender and sexuality, a clear delineation between *sex* and *gender* is typically prescribed, with *sex* as the preferred term for biological forms, and *gender* limited to its meanings involving behavioral, cultural, and psychological traits (WFW follows this concept).

<u>He</u>: Used in a generic sense or **when the gender of the person is unspecified.** (Note from the author: You will see a discussion on this as you read forward. Using "he" to include both sexes must end; indeed, it has already been replaced in most cases by "he/she" or "they." Read what WFW has done to resolve this problem in Chapter 8).

<u>Human</u>: A person. (Note from the author: If there's any word that tells us English is a "man's" language, it's hu**man**.)

<u>Male</u>: An individual of the sex that is typically capable of producing small, usually mobile, gametes (such as sperm or spermatozoa) that fertilize the eggs of a female.

<u>Man</u>: *Especially* an adult male human. <u>Woman</u>: *Especially* an adult female human.

WFW Definitions

NOTE: WFW defines the two primary sexes (men and women) "by birth or preference." In dealing with issues of equality, we only focus on the inequality between these two. See the dictionary definitions below.

<u>Gendered words</u>: Any English words that, by sound or spelling, suggest a specific sex, especially when no specific sex is intended. WFW discusses the 100 most common words in English, of which 16 words exhibit this characteristic—that's 16%!

<u>"He" words</u>: Any words in English that use "man," "men," "he," "his," or "him" in sound or spelling. "Sir" and "guy" are additional examples.

<u>"She/her" words</u>: Oh dear! "She" and "her" are already "he" words, so we can't include them. Read on to see what WFW does to fix these!

(WFW is a process used to determine the "he" code of English words. Learn how it works in Chapter 11).

***

This book, which focuses on English words, intends to show how English greatly prefers the term "man," as defined above, and largely ignores what is known as "woman" by offering a few, if any, words to describe ourselves.

I consider Breaking The Bias of English (BTBOE) as a thesis, characterized as "a proposition to be proved or one advanced without proof." I have done my best to reveal what I have observed while taking on the challenge to bring English into a more equitable balance by making a few changes. This book does not intend to be a discourse for any other purpose or definition but rather focuses on the inequalities between our two sexes within the framework of the English language, which robs women of power through its very words.

NOTE: Those who believe that no inequality exists between "man" and those whom English terms "woman" might also be interested in this study, which shows not only how deeply this inequality lies in our words and humanity but also how easily we can choose to bring equality to both.

This book asks readers to consider several essential questions: How can we have equality when so <u>man</u>y words that refer to "wo<u>men</u>" require us to use "he" words? Why does English contain thousands of "he" and so few words for us? More importantly, what can we do to equalize our language?

If such questions beg for your attention, read on.

WEnglish...for WEquality™

Introduction to WEnglish
for WEquality

WEnglish for WEquality (WFW) is the work of a tireless linguist who was shown years ago that English contains thousands of gendered words that are almost entirely masculine and that there are very few words for women.[1] While most of us know that "he" words are common in what is now considered the most commonly spoken tongue in the world, I believe we don't know how many gendered words exist. Hence, it's time to raise awareness so that we can easily fix them.

English "he" words are subliminally dominating our language. We don't realize that English has so few words for us that it can hardly be considered a neutral language, despite the widespread belief that it is. As a linguist, I aim to make English also work for those of us who don't identify as men. Thus, I began my quest to make English an equal and balanced language. Fifteen years later, *Breaking The Bias of English* (BTBOE) is finally being published.

---

[1] Except where otherwise indicated, "we," "us," and "our" refer to women, whether by birth or preference. A notable exception: Chapter 9, which deals with pronouns

Within these pages, you'll discover how masculine English is, and I'll show you, from a linguist's perspective, how simple it is to rectify it. English must respect us equally to become a "we" language, drawing us together with words in a way previously unknown to us. Therefore, my mission and motto is "WEnglish for WEquality."

While this is my "work," it stems from the realm of ideas, much like everything else. I've accepted the knowledge, and I'm now sharing it with you. What you do with it is up to you. However, I hope you will embrace the concept because its importance cannot be overstated. Women must attain equality in the world's most common language.[2]

To clarify, while Mandarin Chinese has the largest number of native speakers, English holds the top spot as the most commonly spoken language because of its prevalent use as a second language.

Isn't the desire for equality universal, even when people have differing opinions on issues? Aren't we weary of using war, politics, blame, and divergent views to determine who's responsible for the troubles in our world? In the United States alone, members of both sexes battled for years until equal voting rights were achieved. Yet now, over 100 years later, women still don't enjoy equal rights in other significant aspects of life.

Note to the readers: If you believe that equality between our sexes isn't an issue or that English is fine as it is, this book may not be for you. But please feel free to read on, as it may provide some valuable insights. *BTBOE* assumes that its readers agree that our world (indeed, our own country) faces challenges regarding equality, where men are *still* preferred over women in almost every way. I appreciate both sexes and simply want to establish equality in English.

---

[2]   https://www.statista.com/statistics/266808/the-most-spoken-languages-worldwide/

The Power of WE

"We" is the goal of WFW—a vision to draw us together in a unique way, using words to recognize each person's unique gifts and individuality. Our world is becoming increasingly fractured, with countries still at war and innocent lives being lost. Why? Do we not desire an end to such suffering?

We are not powerless. Let me show you how a few word changes in English can bring us closer to unity. Do words possess that kind of power? According to some of our world's wise ones, yes. Even the Bible says, "The tongue is mightier than the sword" (sword is "word" with an s in front of it). "Unite" can also be rearranged to spell "untie." We must decide what we want and act to make changes that can create a better world.

I am not claiming that changing six words will bring world peace. I am offering a concept that equalizes our world's most common language to bring balance and honor to both men and women. It's easy to do. The question is, *will we?*

Why Read This Book?

This book...

Offers a way to neutralize English with just **one** word, thereby diminishing its intense preference for "he" words, giving women, by birth or preference, the freedom to choose words that resonate with their identity.

Shows how English words have robbed those who are not men of word power by inundating English with "he" words. It demonstrates how we can create a language of equality by neutralizing English and establishing five words of our own.

Awakens women to the realization that our centuries of using male-centric words have kept us captive. It empowers us to become free at last.

Gives us an easy way to recognize and detach from words that subtly affect us, making us feel invisible and unheard.

Reminds us of the power of words and how *difficult it is to be equal without words of our own* to express who we are in our own voices.

Finally, this is a book I have written with great joy while uncovering how words can help us attain equality within the English language.

Welcome to WEnglish for WEquality (WFW)

Chapter 1

The Word That Shined on Me

"I know nothing in the world that has as much power as a word. Sometimes, I write one, and I look at it until it begins to shine."

—Emily Dickinson[3]

It was August 2008. I was happily working on the fifth story of my novel series, *The Avery Victoria Spencer Fables*, which remains capped at four books[4] because I took a stunning detour to excavate and refurbish English, an ancient language that has perpetually dishonored and disempowered women. For eons, men have appeared fearful of sharing equality with us.

Trained as a linguist and immersed in novel writing, I have made a wonderful living by teaching affordable housing tax regulations for over thirty years, which requires deep research and knowledge. That, for me, was pure joy. I cannot bear to ignore things I do not understand, so I dig deep into whatever interests me, and while writing fiction, I almost exclusively read non-fiction for its ability to stimulate my imagination.

This also holds for my works of fiction. I write what I'm given, and plots get so interesting that I can't stop (just ask my loving husband of 37 years.) I don't use an outline; I let my imagination narrate the story

---

3   Emily Dickinson, Quotes by Emily Dickinson, *Goodreads* (2023) ttps:// www.goodreads. com/quotes/82436

4   Vivian Probst, *The Avery Victoria Spencer Fables*, a 4–book fictional series

it wants me to write, acting like a secretary. However, the plot often doesn't come to me systematically. Most of my novels come to me in pieces, and I watch them magically snap into place when the story is complete. That's what I was doing when I saw the periodic table of elements (PTE) while working on Book Five.

I have always let characters and plots show up on their own. I don't create outlines or try to conjure up compelling narratives. And while I'm no Stephen King, I agree with his belief that "…stories pretty much make themselves. The job of the writer is to give them a place to grow."[5] His narratives are so admirable that if you're a writer (whether fiction or nonfiction), you need to take him seriously.

My venture into novel writing life began with a dream on March 10, 2000. Writing fiction became a part of my busy life until I retired from my consulting business in 2020 (see my novels at vivianprobst.com). Since BTBOE marks a departure into non-fiction, it is challenging. Stephen King aptly calls non-fiction "torture" because it must be factual and is less creative. Nevertheless, when I received my stroke of insight, my heart knew what to do.

Upon retirement, I could focus more on writing. I love the word "retired," which makes me think of putting new tires on a car to keep moving forward in life. BTBOE took a prominent position at this time as a "front runner." I was committed and excited, ready to go full steam ahead.

My original goal was to finish Book Five of the AVS series, which I had begun, but I ended up taking a massive detour because of a simple element on the periodic table.

I was also determined to keep an open mind, ensuring I didn't blame anyone for the bias in the English language. While acknowledging our culture's patriarchal history, I wanted to avoid focusing on it. My

---

[5] Stephen King, *On Writing* (200); Scribner, p. 163.

objective was to point out English's ancient errors from a woman's viewpoint and find a way to transform it into a language of equality. Over time, I was shown easy ways to do that. In fact, I marveled at the simple word changes that could have such a huge impact and be used to foster equality in English.

I worked on this book for about two years, and it wasn't easy to stay on task. Despite deliberately keeping readership low to stay true to myself, staying away from the vast landscape of gender issues was challenging.

That's why I said what I did at the beginning of this book.

While writing Book Five, I felt compelled to include my mysterious late Uncle Van as a character. That was a first—writing about someone I knew.

As a child, I'd heard he was a sort of genius—he had been studying "cold fusion" in college and had been dedicated to reorganizing the periodic table—until "something happened." I assumed it was a mental breakdown because my family never talked about it, except once when I was about twelve years old.

I had stayed overnight at a friend's pajama party. We played a game with a mirror called "I See Mary Merriweather." After I explained how it worked to my father (say her name three times and then look in a mirror. If you see her, it's supposed to mean something. But I didn't see her), he proceeded to scold me, making me promise to never do it again. "It's from the devil, and it's what affected your Uncle Van." My father was not a stern man, so I knew it was a serious matter, and I made a promise.

The aftermath of my uncle's trauma led him to leave a promising future and return to his family home in the wheatfields of Saskatchewan, Canada, where he remained for the rest of his life. Decades later, I wanted to dig out the details, maybe even reinvent the periodic table in his honor. When it's fiction, you can do what you want to.

I gleefully began studying and playing with the PTE to see how I could make a story out of it. I know it sounds preposterous, but fiction makes these ideas fun to play with. However, I didn't get to play for very long. Everything came to a screeching halt when I saw the second element, "He" (the symbol for Helium). Yes, the word shined on me, but it was more like a blinding flash that changed my life's trajectory. My entire focus shifted to that one word as my mind raced down an entirely new thought track. Yes, you might say that "He" shined on me and that it's been doing so ever since.

Where are the words for those of us who aren't men? I asked myself, thinking it would be a lark to follow that train of thought. But the train never left the station because I couldn't match the many "he" words in English with any "non-he" words. It stunned me. Sure, I already vaguely knew that English had more words for men than for women, but I'd never studied its impact. Even "she" contains "he," so it's also a "he" word.

During my consulting career, I traveled quite a lot, so I had plenty of time to scrutinize English words. I'd circle "he" words in the books I read and try to find a few words for us, but they were few and mostly linked to men.

"Am I out of my mind?" I asked myself relentlessly (and still do). But the resounding answer has always been, "No, Vivian, you're seeing English as it really is, and now, you can fix it." It's time for us to ask:

Why does English have so few words for those of us known as "wo-men"? Why do the most common words for us link us to men: wo-<u>men</u>, wo<u>man</u>, <u>she</u>, <u>her</u>, fe<u>male</u>? We need to ask these questions before deciding whether we care or not because I believe we're becoming increasingly invisible in our world.

Could our lack of equality actually be a lexical issue? Is English subliminally responsible for our inability to progress toward equal? Can we neutralize the language to make it work for both sexes? Indeed, can we make English a fair and equal "we language," with words for both sexes instead of over 20,000 for men and so few for us? Seeing the problem was only the beginning. It became my passion to fix it.

To say I was blown away by these thoughts would be an understatement. My linguistic word world shook and trembled as if I had unearthed a groundbreaking discovery. *Could it be true? Was our lack of words for us laying the bedrock of our inequality?*

I knew I had to leave my world of fiction behind. What I had discovered was too important to ignore—it needed to be shared.

In her book, *A Stroke of Insight*, Jill Bolte Taylor recounts her rather sudden physical stroke, detailing how she could understand what was happening to her brain and miraculously move through it with the support of others, thereby saving her life and giving us new insights into how our brains work. The outcome? More inner peace, compassion, and joy, which she shares around the world.[6]

Reflect on the word, "<u>insight</u>," because it explains where everything in life really begins—not inside our physical bodies but in the realm of thoughts and ideas. These *insights* (revelations, inventions, curiosities, and new understandings) come to us from *somewhere*, giving us clues to our purpose and direction in life on Earth. Often, we are tasked with

---

[6] Jill Bolte Taylor, *My Stroke of Insight* (2009), Penguin Books

studying and searching for our "calling" with the clues we are given. That's the approach I adopted when "He" showed up.

We are not here to roam without direction or purpose. Rather, as we interact with what our minds, through our thoughts, reveal to us, we can uncover the work and purpose we have been gifted with. Too often, we ignore the ideas that come to us instead of "injoying" where they lead. We might write these off as "foolishness" when we need to embrace them.

There Are No Mistakes, Just Lessons to Be Learned

I didn't experience a physical stroke like Bolte Tayor did, but the word "He" seized my attention so forcefully that I turned from writing fiction to researching English. Yes, the word that is also the second element on the PTE creates thousands of words in English—even words for us such as "she" and "her."

Vivian's backstory: For those interested in knowing my backstory, you can find it at the back of this book to peruse at your convenience. It's a condensed version because I don't think it's vital to this book. You can read it and decide for yourself. Or you can read my memoir, *I Was a Yo-Yo Wife...Until I Learned THIS!* "This" saved me and my marriage by introducing me to "meology"—the study of me, an important exploration for each of us to undertake to understand ourselves.

Chapter 2

Breaking the English "He" Code

Willing to Be a Fool

Breaking codes isn't for the faint of heart—it demands a willingness to be a fool. In his mesmerizing recounting of how the Allies finally deciphered the German codes, leading to the end of World War II, Simon Singh[7] takes readers on a thrilling ride into how secret codes were broken, especially during wartime. It's almost unbelievable how deep codebreakers had to delve to find these "code keys" and make sense of them. Yet, when matters of life and death are at stake, code breakers have done what otherwise appears impossible.

From Singh's book:

Two such analysts were Whitfied Diffie and Martin Hellman, both grappled to solve a cryptographer's nightmare: physically transporting keys (code breakers) across vast distances. It felt like an impossible dream until Ralph Merkle joined the duo. (Author's note: Please remember this was long before we had the internet and computers.)

Martin Hellman notes, "Ralph Merkle, like us, was willing to be a fool. And the way to get to the top of the heap in terms of developing original research is to be a fool because _only fools keep trying_....Unless you're foolish enough to be continually excited, you won't have the motivation, you won't have the energy to carry it through. God rewards fools."

---

[7]   Simon Singh, *The Code Book: The Science of Secrecy from Ancient Egypt to Quantum Cryptography* (1999), Anchor Books, p. 256

Another trait of fools, Hellman says, is that "fools don't care about failure; every step leads to eventual discovery."

No one refers to Edison, Einstein, Marie Curie, Grace Hopper, and other inventors and discoverers as "fools." In fact, Einstein once remarked, "It's not that I'm so smart, I just stick with the problem longer."[8] And he did, as did many women who worked behind the scenes on some important discoveries, working diligently and contributing ideas and research without recognition.

Recently, I learned about Cecilia Payne-Gaposchkin, who changed the world by introducing a new concept to science. She is credited with determining the composition of stars.[9] I'm pleased that we are finally recognizing the hundreds, perhaps thousands of women who have impacted our world. More books and movies (like *Hidden Figures*)[10] are giving belated credit to women's accomplishments. I want to commend those who are finally writing these stories, as it is another critical step on our journey to equality.

The takeaway? Codebreakers don't give up. Watch the movie *The Imitation Game* for a dramatic portrayal of codebreaking, which also credits a woman for suggesting the solution.[11] Indeed, a significant number of women worked tirelessly (and without credit) behind the scenes, doing the hard work during the Enigma project.

I'm alright with being a fool for English. This idea has supported me while wading through words for years, looking for ways to give us

[8] Albert Einstein, *Brainy Quotes*, (2023) https://www.brainyquote.com/quotes/albert_ein stein_106192

[9] Donovan Moore, *What Stars are Made Of: The Life of Cecilia Payne-Gaposchkin* (2020), Harvard University Press

[10] Shetterly, Margot Lee, *Hidden Figures: The American Dream and the Untold Story of the Blak Women Mathematicians Who Helped Win the Space Race* (2016), William Morrow Paperbacks

[11] Jason Fagone, *The Woman Who Smashed Codes* (2017), Dey St.

words of our own. Yes, I've felt like a fool but a happy one with a true sense of purpose. I refuse to give up and with good reason—I believe I've found the secret key code to equalize English.

I Take On The Challenge

"Language conveys a certain power. It is one of the instruments of domination. It is carefully guarded by the superior people because it is one of the means through which they conserve their supremacy."

—Sheila Rowbotham[12]

"Superior," "supremacy"—these are powerful words, yet you will find them appropriate once you see what I've learned about English words.

Being a linguist[13] and an equalist,[14] seeing "He" on the periodic table challenged me to search for *any* strong English words for us. It didn't take me long to realize there are none (yet).[15]

---

[12] Sheila Rowbotham, English socialist feminist theorist and historian, Top Sheila Rowbotham Quotes, (2023) quotefancy.com

[13] A **linguist** is someone who engages in the academic discipline of linguistics. Due to social and institutional forces, women in linguistics have been marginalized, generating significant interest in both the causes of and solutions to gender bias in linguistics.

[14] Feminism and equalism are two powerful social movements that advocate for equality and equal rights. While **feminists take a women-centered approach, equalists rise above all social categorization, advocating for universal equality for all.**

[15] "He" words include "he," "him," "his," "man," "men," "sir," and "guy."

Chapter 3

The Word Science Behind WFW

English has fascinated and perplexed me for years. I've used a variety of tools that you can also employ to conduct your own English word analysis to dive deeper than the few words we discuss here. There are so <u>many</u> hidden "he" codes in English.

If you like word games, you'll find WFW fun, which isn't the goal, of course. Once you start working with word splits, twists, and colliders,[16] you'll probably find yourself laughing out loud on occasion. You'll see all of this shortly.

What is The WEnglish Word Collider?

The WEnglish Word Collider, like the CERN Large Hadron Collider (LHC) that blasts particles apart to find the smallest units of power, blasts words apart into letters to reveal their smallest energy particles. This process is much easier than the LHC since our "colliders" reside within our brains.

---

[16] The Large Hadron Collider (LHC), built by CERN, is the world's largest and most powerful particle accelerator. It consists of a 27-kilometer ring of superconducting magnets with numerous accelerating structures to boost the energy of the particles along the way. See www.home.cern/science/accelerators/large-hadron-collider.

Sample Use of The WEnglish Word Collider: Blame

My personal favorite word to split into particles, "blame", shows us how intricately English can code words. It's also important to recognize the coded nature of these words as we read and write them, without making it a horrendous challenge. Let's explore what we can uncover with this particular English word code.

Step 1 (optional): Study the etymology of the word, which you can do at your leisure. You'll see how word origins can undergo complete transformations over time. "Blame" originates from the Latin word "culp", from which we derive "culpable."

Step 2: Split into syllables if possible. "Blame" is a single-syllable word that cannot be split by syllable but by obvious connotation, and humorously so, into "b-lame." I like to say that "blame makes us lame," which, I believe, understates the impact of the word on our world.

Step 3: What other words can be spelled with these letters? This is where things get interesting. See what other words you can come up with, but be careful to use only the letters in the word. This isn't SCRABBLE, and there are no blank letters or other letters to connect to.

Step 4: Is "blame" a "he" word? At first glance, no. But on playing with the letter positions, the word "male" comes up. Isn't that interesting? However, since WFW only considers words that are obviously "he" words, we don't count "blame" as a "he" word, though you could if you wish to. The fact that those of us who aren't men tend to *blame* men for various issues (and vice versa) does not convince us that it's a "he" word, as humorous as that thought may be.

Try Another Word: Equality

Step 1 (optional): Google informs us that "equality" comes from the Middle French word "equalité," descending from the Latin "aequalitas," with meanings that are essentially identical across the millennia, referring to the sameness of amount as well as of status or shape. It's clear that this word's meaning hasn't changed much over time.

Step 2: Equality has four syllables—E-qual-i-ty.

What other words can be found in e-qual-i-ty? A few jump right out—equal, quality, all. Isn't that interesting? Do we think of "quality" when we use that word? What about "all"? Yes, it's spelled with only one "l," but if you say it out loud, it sounds like "all." That's pretty powerful when we stop and think about it!

Step 3: What other words can be spelled with "equality"? You're on your own here, but remember our rule is different than Scrabble. You can use letters in the word multiple times, but you can't connect to any others. Wordmaker.com came up with 88 words!

Step 4: Is Equality a "he" word? No.

We could go on with more words using this process (and yes, "this" is a "he" word), but we need to get to our next important point.

Remember our six words: The, She, Her, Woman, Wimin, They. As mentioned, "this" is also a "he" word, but we will not be focusing on it. You can change it or substitute it, but I hope you're okay if we pass on this one. There are numerous others will not be discussing. Why? Because we believe it only takes our *six words* to turn English into a balanced language.

Do Word Changes Make Us Uncomfortable?

I recall discussing with a woman how English disempowers us, and she said, "I know what you're saying is true, but I just try not to think about it." I say, let's do more than avoid thinking about it because it makes a difference to all of us, and we need more powerful words for ourselves. Let's embrace a few words for ourselves because, damn it (is "damn" a "he" word? Oh, yes. Okay, "darn" it), we have that right! It's easier and more peaceful to fix words than to rant our way to power. Changing a few words is a gentle approach.

Chapter 4

How English Keeps Us Trapped

The "He" Word Chart

Attempting to quantify the number of "he" words that are spelled in a controlled order of letters in the vast realm of the internet is a mind-boggling task, but we've done our very best. However, we've noted that words for women commonly attach us to men, as shown below:

"Wo" + men = women
"Fe" + male = female
"S" + he = she
"He"+r = her

We all "sort of" know this, but we haven't observed its impact on us. We joke about it when we should be truly outraged. Personally, I wouldn't have been aware of this if I hadn't been studying my late uncle's work. Yes, we're attached—too attached—to "he" words.

Look at the following chart and see for yourself.

Regardless of the internet website used (we opted for The Free Dictionary by Farlex because a] it's fairly reliable and b] yes, it's free), the results remain consistent. The six most common words representing us use "he" words (see Column 3). That's why there is a zero in each column for "our words." We are seemingly invisible! Note that while these six words are the most common in English for us, they are not "common words" at all (see Chapter Four).

The "He" Word Chart

'HE' Words		'OUR' Words	
1	2	3	4
	# of English Words		# of English Words
He	8,270	She*	0
Man	2,148	Wo*man*	0
Men**	2.539	Wo*men*	0
Him/*Hym*	238	*Her*	0
His	2,039	*Hers*	0
Male	183	Fe*male*	0
Subtotal	15,417		0
Guy	203		
Sir	592		
Cer**	3,004		
Total	19,216		0

English has *thousands* of "he" words. The chart above shows all the "he" words considered in this book. Notably, there are *no words* in English for us that do not link us to men. That's why there are zeros in Column 4 of the above chart. You'll see more about this when we delve into the 100 most common words in English in Chapter Four. Observe how English words work, and then let's work together to change it.

Some common questions that come up when discussing this chart are:

What if we don't feel like changing any words in English? What's the downside?

I respond to this with a different question: *How can we be equal if we have no words of our own?* That's been my endeavor—to find a way to fix English because words wield immense power, and our lack of words of our own diminishes our power.

Women have endured this power imbalance for eons, and it's time to fix that. Sadly, some individuals in high positions believe that English is gender-neutral. This is simply not true. My mission is to raise awareness so that we can make informed choices about what to do.

Can equality really hang in the balance because of English words?

If you think this is impossible, you're not alone, but you're in the wrong camp. I, too, was oblivious and indifferent to this English word predicament. Even after discovering it, I hesitated to share it, even after I started my linguistic excavation. Yet, the concept would not leave me alone. I had to pursue it, even when I doubted myself.

The deeper I dug, the more convinced I was that I needed to share what I'd learned with others. The outcome? We can unite to make English a language that serves everyone. Remember, that's why "we" is so important in "WEnglish for WEquality."

Put simply, if we want to have words of our own, we must choose to create and use a few English words differently. But slow down and breathe. Let's not make this a "free for all" campaign that would create chaos. Let's agree on the words we choose to change so that these changes coalesce into empowerment.

Word Substitutions

Here's another brilliantly easy idea to pull some "he" words out of English. You don't need formal instruction for this at all. While writing, if you come across a word with "he" in it, you can decide whether to use it or not. If you believe that words have power (and they do) and that the words we use make a difference (and they do), simply opt for a different word. It's that easy.

WFW is altering six words because they are so common and vital that substituting them for other words wouldn't suffice. I understand as well as you do that no one wants to go through the hassle of altering the spelling of English words just because they contain "he." Therefore, except for the few changes WFW makes, simply choose a different word. That's how we can turn English into a language of equality.

Some individuals argue that we do indeed have a few words representing us, such as girl, daughter, wife, aunt, and queen. These are primarily relational and not common outside those specific contexts.

Chapter 5

More Stunning Proof—The 100 Most Common Words in English

After that startling revelation of the prevalence of "he" words, I began reading book after book, counting every occurrence of "he" words. Guess what! *Ten to twelve percent of English words are "he" words!*[17] While I was stunned by the sheer volume of "he" words in English, it didn't really impact me until I found a way to analyze the most common words. Once I saw *that* list, my vision to make English work for all of us multiplied exponentially. Although most of us don't perceive English as offensive, I believe that deep in our souls, we sense exclusion and feel offended.

I thought it would be easy to find a source on the internet for the 100 most common words in English. However, my exploration only led to more confusion. Different groups had different opinions and agendas, resulting in a focus on different concepts. However, there was a general consensus on the 100 most common words. Having studied multiple lists and data, I've found minimal differences in the first 100 words, with the "he" words dominating.

Look at the chart above. These are the 100 commonest (which is a correct word if you're British) words written in English based on the billion-word Oxford English Corpus (OEC).[18] We've made it easy to pick out the "he" words by highlighting them in **bold.**

---

[17] Five to seven percent are based on the word "the" alone.

[18] Based on the Oxford English Dictionary https://www.englishclub.com/

1. the	21. at	41. there	61. some	81. my
2. of	22. be	42. use	62. her	82. than
3. and	23. this	43. an	63. would	83. first
4. a	24. have	44. each	64. make	84. water
5. to	25. from	45. which	65. like	85. been
6. in	26. or	46. she	66. him	86. call
7. is	27. one	47. do	67. into	87. who
8. you	28. had	48. how	68. time	88. oil
9. that	29. by	49. their	69. has	89. its
10. it	30. word	50. if	70. look	90. now
11. he	31. but	51. will	71. two	91. find
12. was	32. not	52. up	72. more	92. long
13. for	33. what	53. other	73. write	93. down
14. on	34. all	54. about	74. go	94. day
15. are	35. were	55. out	75. see	95. did
16. as	36. we	56. many	76. number	96. get
17. with	37. when	57. then	77. no	97. come
18. his	38. your	58. them	78. way	98. made
19. they	39. can	59. these	79. could	99. may
20. I	40. said	60. so	80. people	100. part

You can also consult a word list at the Corpus of Contemporary American English (COCA) or visit espressoenglish.com, among several other websites. Ensure that any list you study is based on how often that word is used in English. Some lists are alphabetical and some are categorized by type, such as adjective or noun—both don't work for WFW. Wikipedia uses the same list as the OEC, which contains over two billion English words.[19] If that doesn't impress you, it should.

These 100 most common words in English are outrageously telling. Look at the prevalence of "he" words—sixteen out of 100, which is 16%. And the words for women? None. Even the two words in this

vocabulary/com mon-words-100.php.

[19] https://www.oxfordreference.com/abstract/acref

list that could be "ours" are really "he" words. "S<u>he</u>" (#46) and "<u>her</u>" (#62) are both considered "he" words by WFW. We've gotta fix that! And it's easy, as you will soon see.

Here's what's most important: It doesn't matter which word list you examine. If you scrutinize lists of the most commonly used words in English *in order of usage*, you'll see "the" consistently at the top. We'll address neutralizing that word shortly.

Does any of this evidence convince you that we're shunned by English?

Have you noticed how angry and outspoken some of us have become? Often, we're not entirely sure why. Many of us don't identify with June Cleaver anymore. We want to be seen and respected for our individual gifts and talents, seeking more rights and influence on issues that matter to us. Mostly, we want to be treated fairly and recognized for the impact we've always had on our world. The absence of words for us could be an undiscovered and underlying reason, long trapped in the bedrock of English.

Am I alone in feeling tired of men running societal structures—of centuries of war, death, rape, and other crimes of "subservience" and being labeled "less than" when we know we're not? We possess intellect, and we want to be respected for using it rather than playing a role that others (i.e., mostly men from centuries ago) decided we were restricted to. Yes, we finally got the right to vote after a century-long struggle. However, there's so much more we deserve credit for and so much more we can do to shape a "we" world of peaceful cooperation.

Are we now realizing how English excludes us? Have we considered how our language robs us of our power? As a seasoned linguist, I decided someone should take this on, and since I couldn't find anyone else doing it exactly this way and because of how I discovered it, I felt inspired and compelled to dive in.

Chapter 6

Why It's Important to Break the Bias NOW

"Gender biases have existed in language ostensibly forever, but only now does English-speaking culture find itself in the position to make a language revolution happen… <u>*for the first time in history,*</u> *we have both the concrete linguistic data and the emotional momentum to inspire tangible differences in how we talk about gender*[20] *and how we perceive the speech of men, women, and everyone in between.*

(Emphasis by author)."[21]

"Concrete linguistic data and emotional momentum"—watch how WFW channels that energy into tangible results. It's time to fix this!

Right now, our world is becoming more conscious of the need to foster greater equality for women. Therefore, we must press forward *now* because we can.

Most women are becoming leaders in their fields of interest: more of us are earning college and doctorate degrees; running for government

---

[20] Writers often interchange "sex" and "gender." WFW clearly separates these because "sex" has only two primary categories, and that's what this book is about.

[21] Amanda Montell in her 2019 book *Wordslut: A Feminist Guide to Taking Back the English Language*. Don't you love that her last name has "tell" in it?

positions; becoming doctors, lawyers, scientists, and researchers; and pioneering innovative business models. Our influence is expanding, and more men are joining our ranks as they embrace the principles of equality for all (notice that we say "al" in equality).

The UN's HeForShe movement, operational since 2014, has been bringing women from developing, male-dominated countries into leadership and international corporations. Let's ride this wave to equality! By reshaping English to be inclusive for all, we're breaking one of the most stubborn strongholds that ever existed.

***

Some people think my stance is ridiculous. "Vivian, six words can't resolve our issues with equality." I agree. Are you surprised? I know that nothing can change unless we *act*. If we let English words continue to inflict their power over us, we're in trouble. It only takes a few people to "get it" and become a force for change.

Case in point: the few women who took down Harvey Weinstein. Their act demanded incredible guts and courage, but they stepped forward and opened that door, giving women an opportunity to choose to tell the truth without reprisal—which is critical to equality. It's a sign that we're ready, and the time is now.

The late Margaret Mead (1901–1978), a famous anthropologist, once said, *"Never doubt that a small group of thoughtful, committed citizens can change the world. Indeed, it's the only thing that ever has."* We can do this.

Let's Overcome the Effects of Patriarchy

"The truth may set you free, but first, it will shatter the safe, sweet way you live."[22]

---

[22] Sue Monk Kidd, *Dance of the Dissident Daughter (1996)*, HarperOne, pg. 15.

Have you had such an experience? Sue Monk Kidd did as she realized how patriarchy influenced her deepest, most sacred beliefs about god, who, in her upbringing, had always been referred to as "he." She bravely changed her perspective and began to open up to a goddess experience. Yes, it takes courage to move out of patriarchy. She has shared her journey publicly in her book, *Dance of the Dissident Daughter*.[23]

I had a similar experience that required me to leave a lifestyle that had conditioned me to be submissive to men. After seven years of missionary training, married with two young children, my first husband and I went to Africa to convert "primitive tribal people" to Christianity. But *I* was the one who was converted.

There, under a mosquito net at night, I wrestled for six months after realizing that that was not my life or my calling. Rather, I was following what I had been taught, following my parents' path. The problem with walking in someone else's footprints is that we leave none of our own. In anguish and poor health, I left everything—my heritage, my family, my beliefs, and my social culture—to begin living an honest life and become true to my calling.

You might not be in a position where your life decisions necessitate a change in the "safe, sweet way you live" as Sue Monk Kidd describes it. Changing a few words in English also shouldn't have that effect. After all, "the sky is not falling."

But rumor has it that people generally don't like change. I've witnessed people respond to my work with English—first, the shock, frowns, and protests, followed by growing awareness and sometimes smiles that indicate understanding. Little by little, I've seen doors of awareness open.

Look at how long patriarchy has ruled! Wait, let's change that into the past tense—"Look at how long patriarchy *ruled*!" English words have been shattering our lives for centuries! We were unconscious of this

---

[23] Ibid.

because they are so subliminally entrenched in our culture that even now, people are shocked to discover how masculine English is.

***

It's important to realize with "real eyes" that *every time we see a "he" word (even if these appear inside other words, as they do in thousands of English words)*, we can't ignore that "he" is *always preferred* in English. How can our entire sex be missing? Look at how women are being treated after all these years. Could the absence of words for us be a root cause? Let's delve deeper and fix it!

Dr. Leonard Shlain extensively studied the impact of words on women, examining the effect of literacy on cultures that had been matriarchal for centuries. He observed how words (left-brain activity) influenced their societies, creating a male-dominant culture wherever it was introduced. He hypothesized that "when a critical mass of people within a society acquire literacy, especially alphabet literacy, left hemispheric modes of thought are reinforced at the expense of right hemispheric ones, which manifests as a decline in the status of images, women's rights, and goddess worship."[24]

Shlain illustrates his discovery in over four hundred pages, moving from culture to culture and carefully confirming his theory. In his epilogue, he concludes, "Learning to spell occurs at such a young age that people are unaware of the changes in perception it causes. Once a person learns the alphabet, their mental processes will influence their every assumption and decision for the rest of their lives."[25]

Consider all the areas where one sex has majority control in our world, our cultures, and our countries. We need to consider how our own words influence that control because each time we use the word "he"

---

[24] Dr. Leonard Shlain, *The Alphabet Versus the Goddess: The Conflict Between Word and Image* (1998), Penguin/Compass, Preface, p. 2.

[25] Ibid., p. 429.

in any form, our brains register "men." You'll see how simple it is to undo the "he" influence of English and, in that way, untie ourselves from words that keep us bound.

Let's unite to free ourselves from patriarchal English. Fixing this problem could make a pivotal difference—the difference—in balancing our world and equalizing our role in it, but we must acknowledge how it's been affecting each of us individually. *We must assert our own power to reshape our world by transforming our words.*

This transformation is already happening in some countries.[26] According to a 2023 article by Katharina Buchholtz, fourteen countries have achieved this goal, but the United States has not been listed among them. Why not? Shouldn't we be leading the charge?

What's stopping us? Why are we still confined to lower-paying jobs? Is there a deeper issue at play—that we don't feel worthy—or are we just not interested in seeking more influence and power? Critical self-honesty is required if we want anything to change.

Equalizing Brain Power

One issue that has proven tough to overcome is the belief among many of us that we are "less than" men—that even our brains are designed for "other, lesser work." Is this perception accurate? Not at all! With changing gender roles, we're witnessing that our brains function just as effectively as men's brains,[27] perhaps in different ways. If we believe

---

[26] Only 14 countries in the world offer full legal protections to women, according to the report *Women, Business and the Law, 2023*, recently published by the World Bank. Belgium, Canada, Denmark, France, Greece, Iceland, Ireland, Latvia, Luxembourg, Portugal, Spain, and Sweden, as well as Germany and the Netherlands, offer full equal rights to men and women, at least from a legal perspective. https://www.statista.com/chart/17290/ countries-with-most-equal-rights-for-women/

[27] Valeria Maltoni, *Are Men's and Women's Brains Different?* http://www.

our brains are inferior, it can cause us to think that we are less than men—a scary conclusion to draw. Perhaps we simply don't believe we're intellectually gifted. *Is it also possible that some of us don't want to be seen?*

Our brains are incredible, a gift to each of us, so we must accept this gift and use it to its fullest potential. If you want to understand the power of your brain more fully, *Wired for Love* by Stephanie Cacioppo is a wonderful read. Cacioppo is a neuroscientist who has studied the influence of love on brain activity, with results that reassure us that love exists in and nourishes our brains, not our hearts. She has also repeatedly proven that our subliminal minds perceive words much faster than our brains can handle, almost in a "preconscious" manner.[28]

During the upbringing of my generation (Baby Boomers), most of us had to "toe the line" and do things according to our parents' preferences and were often punished if we didn't. Oh, the damage it has done to young people! But our society is changing, and children are increasingly being recognized for their special brilliance, allowing them to find their own place in the world and contribute their creative talents.

As we allow ourselves to explore and express who we really are, archaic roles and beliefs begin to change. We become more comfortable showing our preferences without feeling burdened about them. Let's not be confined by outdated cultural notions that our brains are wired differently[29] unless we unanimously concur that *we are each wired uniquely for our own preferences and talents* and that we should be comfortable enough to share these gifts and talents openly, regardless of sex.

---

conversationa gent.com

[28] Stephanie Cacioppo, *Wired for Love* (2022), Flatiron Books, pp. 58–61

[29] *How Different are Men's and Women's Brains?* Science Daily, March 29, 2021. "Massive study reveals few differences between men's and women's brains."

Our Biggest Challenge

And therein lies our biggest challenge: Who decided that men have particular traits and women have different ones? That we live on different planets? Such a quandary! Our physical sex has *nothing* to do with who we each are. Our different body parts have different functions, yes, but our talents and gifts are specific to each of us, and we must allow ourselves to express these talents in our world and in our words without fear of reprisal. We return to the fundamental concept that each of us is uniquely created, and it's important to respect that rather than compare ourselves or, god forbid, categorize ourselves and make some of us feel like we don't belong.

Our Two Primary Sexes

Yes, we have two primary sexes, each with specific body parts designed for procreation and enjoyment. While there are some exceptions, our purpose here is to talk about men and women in general.

Any divine being who devised sexual intercourse as a procreative activity likely had a sense of humor and a touch of magic. But sex has nothing to do with who we are as individuals. Does that help? The point here is that English words draw positive attention to men and leave us with words that rob us of any sense of importance.

WFW believes that each person is unique, regardless of their genitalia. These two sex categories are useful, yes, but it's time to stop defining people's capabilities and setting behavioral expectations based on what's between their legs. I believe we're finally getting there, but English is yet to catch on.

The late Dr. Leonard Shlain, in his book, used the words "opposite perceptual nodes" (OPN)' to describe our differing interests, talents, and capabilities. To categorize such traits by sex, i.e., confine men and women to specific roles, is a tragedy that has plagued our world for too long. Even Alan Turing, the brilliant mathematician credited with breaking the German "Enigma" code and helping save Britain in World War II, eventually committed suicide, partly because he was forced to undergo hormonal changes to become a woman.

How horrible we have been to those who are perceived as "different" when we should be honoring each of us as unique and important! Leonard Shalin's words, "opposite perceptual nodes," are an unbiased alternative to assigning traits by sex as if we are prepackaged beings.

Shlain was also able to connect the diminishing role of women to the rise of literacy around the world. During his years of research, he proved that "Writing subliminally fosters a patriarchal outlook. Writing of any kind, but especially its alphabetic form, diminishes feminine values and, with them, women's power in the culture."[30] Before ending his book, he expressed his hope that as TV and movies became more prevalent, women would find a more equal footing. However, such has not yet been the case.

---

[30] *The Alphabet Versus the Goddess*, Dr. Leonard Shlain (1998), Penguin/ Compass, Chapter 5

Chapter 7

The Myth of a Genderless English

"If you stand still, there is only one way to go, and that's backwards."

—Peter Shilton[31]

Once again, what often goes unnoticed is the pervasive use of "he" words in our language, which keeps us light years away from a genderless language.

Anyone who has reviewed the 100 most common words list would agree that English has been and still is a man's language that is dominated by "he" words, regardless of efforts to define it otherwise, such as "genderless," "gender neutral," or "gender fair." While these terms are used in specific contexts with specific definitions, it's clear from our research that English remains[32] overtly and subliminally masculine. The book *Unspinning the Spin* has made extraordinary strides in neutralizing the masculine overtones of English.

WFW studies strongly suggest that there's more work to be done. Until English is free of any reference to "he" words, except when referring to men, English *cannot* be considered genderless. It remains entrenched in the patriarchal world we inhabit. We must change words to reverse the trend toward our own invisibility. BTBOE represents a

---

[31] Peter Shilton, a former English soccer player, now a business consultant. https://www. peter-shilton-consultancy.com/

[32] Ibid.

structured initiative to take another important step to "break the bias" and rebalance English, thereby giving us more power to be equal.

Doesn't English Have Plenty of Non-Gendered Words Already? Let's Just Use Those!

Agreed. English has thousands of words that don't specify any gender at all, which are more than those that do. However, our point is that English also contains thousands of common words that overtly favor "he" words. Ignoring these words is no longer an option.

A decision to stop using all existing "he" words would border on mayhem; that's why we've been highly selective and controlled in our efforts. Look at that 100-word list again and try not to use any of the most common "he" words. Ridiculous? Yes. That's why WFW focuses on only six words for targeted change.

Why Do We Use Women's Names for Our Voice/ Personal Assistant Devices?

In today's era, advanced technologies allow us to interact with voice-activated devices. Some of us are old enough to remember the cartoon series "The Jetsons." They had Rosie, remember? Oh, that's right, some of you weren't born back then. Here's a link for a visual reference: https://www.google.com/search?q=picture+of+rosie+from+the+jetsons&oq=Photo+of+Rosie+from+%27The+Je&gs_lcrp=EgZ

We currently have popular voice technologies called "Alexa" or "Siri." Whose idea was it to use women's names? Should we be concerned that we've now reverted to giving orders as if we've gone back at least a century when a woman's place was in the home? Do we think it's funny? Cute? It's not. We ought to use men's names or create genderless names for such systems. Let's stop using women's names. What will artificial intelligence (AI) do to our sex?

Chapter 8

One Word to Neutralize English

"Many problems have solutions that only need to be popularized."[33]

"We need to slow down and understand what English is really saying; we need to start questioning the words we speak every day."[34]

Google (January 9, 2020)

"The most commonly used word in English might only have three letters—but it packs a punch—"the." It's omnipresent; we can't imagine English without it."

Jonathan Culpeper, Professor of Linguistics at Lancaster University, says, *"'The' tops the league tables of most frequently used words in English, accounting for 5% of every 100 words used. 'The' really is miles above everything else."*[35]

"T-h-e" is the most frequently used word in the English language. Studies and analyses of texts have found it to account for at least five percent of all printed English-language words.[36] And that's just *one* word!

---

[33] Robin Morgan, Gloria Steinem, *Unspinning The Spin* (2014)
[34] Amanda Montell, *WORDSLUT* (2019), p. 10
[35] https://www.bbc.com/culture/article/20200109-is-this-the-most-powerful-word-in-the-english-language
[36] Wikipedia and author Vivian Probst, who has studied "the" in English words.

WFW suggests that English treats "t-h-e" in a much more balanced and egalitarian manner because *every time we see "the," we see "he."* This automatic and subliminal association happens so quickly in our brains that we never realized it—until now.

In his seminal work on how language affects women, Dr. Shlian said, "The use of analysis to break each sentence down into its component words, syllables, and letters happens so quickly that it is below awareness."[37] Indeed it is, but once we become aware, we can't help but notice.

Some of us won't be able to read anything ever again without seeing t-h-e leaping off pages, flagging us down, or even waving as we go by because *it now knows that we know.* It's a proud little word, isn't it? It doesn't care that we don't pay it much notice because its real job is to be so subliminal that we don't notice. That way, it hides in plain sight.

The Etymology of "the": "The" and "that" are common developments from the Old English system. Old English had a definite article se (masculine), seo (feminine), and þæt (neuter). In Middle English, these had all merged into þe, the ancestor of the Modern English word "the." https://english.stackexchange.com/questions/11939/what-is-the-etymology-of-the

Note that English once had a masculine, feminine, and neutral form of "the." Now, it only has "the"—a "he" word. Too bad, but we're fixing it. Ready?

Easy Fix #1: Spell It Like It Sounds: THE or THA

Did you know? English speakers often say "t-h-e" in two different ways. Try it here:

---

[37] Leonard Shlian, *The Alphabet vs. The Goddess* (1998), Penguin/Compass, p. 5

The chicken
The egg

Notice any difference?

"The" in "the chicken" is pronounced with a short "a" vowel sound.
"The" in "the egg" is pronounced with a long "e" vowel sound.

You might need to say it a few times, but if you have a good ear, you'll notice it right away. Why does English spell "t-h-e" only one way when we often pronounce it in two different ways? Even if you don't, English does. See below.

According to the Britannica Dictionary:

"There are two ways to pronounce 'the.' One pronunciation sounds like /ðə/ ('thuh,' rhymes with 'duh'), and the other sounds like /ði/ ('thee,' rhymes with 'free'). *The pronunciation of the word 'the' depends on the first sound of the word that comes after it.*"

YouTube can be a valuable resource as well. Here's a useful video, although there are probably hundreds of options to choose from. https://www.youtube.com/watch?app=desktop&v=hTPUJDJqThw

English dictionaries always spell it as "the" and include the alternate pronunciation in parentheses. Why? Is it a plot to add more "he" words and keep us out of English? WFW says probably not, but we're not going to stop here; we're going to address it.

Consider this, if we spell "t-h-e" like it sounds, in most cases, it resolves our "he" word problem! We could spell it in two ways, as "tha"[38]

---

[38] A linguist's phonemic chart uses a symbol called a "pup tent" to create the "a" sound. Since we don't have access to that symbol easily, WFW uses "a." English has over 80,000 words that end in "a" with that same sound. See https://www.thefreedictionary.com/ words-that-end-in-a

chicken and "the" egg. *We'll be adopting this approach throughout tha rest of this book.*

If it feels strange or even objectionable, think about it this way: We already automatically do it with another English article—"a/an."

See tha chart below: The Phonemic Chart

monophthongs				diphthongs		**Phonemic Chart**
						voiced
i:	I	ʊ	u:	Iə	eI	unvoiced
sheep	ship	good	shoot	here	wait	
e	ə	3:	ɔ:	ʊə	ɔI	əʊ
bed	teacher	bird	door	tourist	boy	show
æ	ʌ	ɑ:	ɒ	eə	aI	aʊ
cat	up	far	on	hair	my	cow
p	b	t	d	tʃ	dʒ	k	g
pea	boat	tea	dog	cheese	June	car	go
f	v	θ	ð	s	z	ʃ	ʒ
fly	video	think	this	see	zoo	shall	television
m	n	ŋ	h	l	r	w	j
man	now	sing	hat	love	red	wet	yes

The 44 phonemes of Received Pronunciation based on the popular Adrian Underhill layout   adapted by EnglishClub.com

A phonemic chart is used by linguists to represent sounds with symbols. Most use a more complex chart known as the International Phonetic Alphabet (IPA). By maintaining consistency with tha type of chart used, linguists (especially those working with unwritten languages), ensure uniformity in representing sounds. It's an essential method to guarantee they are consistent with word sounds across different languages or dialects. Interestingly, there are purportedly approximately three thousand unwritten languages left in our world.[39] You'll see how essential this chart is to WFW as we approach English from a "sound" perspective.

---

[39] http://encyclopedia.uia.org/en/problem/149536#:~:text=The%20 majority%20of%20 the%203%2C500,and%20India%20has%20over%20 1%2C000.

Treat T-H-E Like A/AN

English uses two different spellings and pronunciations for a/an, its two non-specific articles. For example:

<u>A chicken</u>

<u>An egg</u>

Can you hear tha difference? Of course! Why don't we say "an chicken" or "a egg"? Because it doesn't sound right, does it? What's going on? Why do we say and write "a/an" as two different words when both mean the same thing? And why don't we do it for "the" when a similar phenomenon is occurring?

Tha general rule for both a/an and the is tha same, but the spelling differs. WFW wants to change that so that both rules align because it's part of how English is taught: use "a" when the indefinite article *precedes* a word beginning with a *consonant* sound and "an" when it precedes a word starting with a *vowel* sound. Now, please don't get all fuzzy-headed about this. If you're reading this book, you've got the brains to cope with a few simple words. Breathe and let's move on. The sky is *not* falling!

We say, "a book" because "b" in "book" is a consonant. We say "an apple" because "a" in "apple" is a vowel. And yes, it's that simple. You might find some exceptions, but that's how English works.

If we apply that same a/an rule to the, we should spell it in two different ways. We will spell it as "tha" before a word that starts with a *consonant* sound, and "the" if tha next word starts with a *vowel.*

Let's try it with our pledge of allegiance, which makes it easier to notice how differently we say "the/tha."

"I pledge allegiance to the/**tha** (circle how you say it) flag of **the**/tha United States of America, and to the/**tha r**epublic for which it stands. One nation, under God, indivisible, with liberty and justice for all."

Ah, if only it were true!

Remember, all we're doing is using tha same technique as a/an. Here are some words for you to practice on:

1) TH__ eagle
2) TH__ plane
3) TH__ alphabet
4) TH__ letter
5) TH__ obstacle
6) TH__ gift

Answer Key: 1=E; 2=A; 3=E; 4=A; 5=E; 6=A

Do we really need to spell "the" in two different ways?

Not unless we persuade dictionaries to change how they spell it. However, let's remember what our objective is here—we want to remove some of the pervasive masculinity embedded in the English language. Since "the" is our most common word (and a "he" word) and we often pronounce it as "tha," we can neutralize English with just one word.

If that was too complicated, consider this: We say "tha" a lot more than we say "the" because English has *twenty-one* consonants and only *five* vowels. This statistic tells us we would say "tha" about 80% of tha time. Hence, we could opt to simply change how we spell and say "the." We should consult dictionaries because, in today's world, it makes sense to make a change universally for linguistic inclusivity.

Can you see what we've accomplished? <u>We just neutralized English with just one word!</u> No muss, no fuss. We've taken tha most common word in English and spelled it as it sounds. That's tha biggest step we can take to remove "he" as our most common gendered word! What a giant leap for us! Our most common "he" word just got fixed, and no one got hurt.

Are You Sure We Should Spell It As "THA"?

Do you believe WFW just decided to change a word's spelling because *we* think it's a good idea? Not at all. There's a rationale behind our new spelling, although Dennis Baron reminds us that "all words are invented."[40]

<u>Did You Know?</u>

There are 44 sounds in English and only 26 letters to spell them.

There are 14 vowel sounds in English and only 6 letters to spell them (if "y" is included).[41] Aha! That explains why we have all these different spelling challenges in English!

Look at the phonemic sound chart below to observe all the symbols used to illustrate different sounds in English and note the circled one.

Tha sound we're looking for is the circled one—"up." That's it. That's tha pup tent we described earlier. Since our computer keyboards make it tricky to create "th^" without some fancy fingerwork, and English doesn't use it in its alphabet, WFW uses an "a."

---

[40] Dennis Baron, *What's Your Pronoun: Beyond He and She*, p. 12

[41] English has around 20 distinct vowel phonemes. This makes it one of the most complex vowel systems of any language in the world. See Babbel. com

	monophthongs				diphthongs			Phonemic Chart
VOWELS	iː sheep	ɪ ship	ʊ good	uː shoot	ɪə here	eɪ wait		voiced unvoiced
	e bed	ə teacher	ɜː bird	ɔː door	ʊə tourist	ɔɪ boy	əʊ show	
	æ cat	ʌ up	ɑː far	ɒ on	eə hair	aɪ my	aʊ cow	
CONSONANTS	p pea	b boat	t tea	d dog	tʃ cheese	dʒ June	k car	g go
	f fly	v video	θ think	ð this	s see	z zoo	ʃ shall	ʒ television
	m man	n now	ŋ sing	h hat	l love	r red	w wet	j yes

The 44 phonemes of Received Pronunciation based on the popular Adrian Underhill layout

adapted by EnglishClub.com

If the idea of using "tha" still bothers you, consider this: English has approximately *eighty-two thousand words that end with "a,"* and most, if not all, use the same "ah" sound, spelled with an "a." WFW decided to stick with what's familiar.

You might see "the" occasionally spelled as "thuh" by others, but if you check how often words are spelled with "uh," you'll understand why WFW sticks with "a."

Are We Insulting Anyone by Changing How We Spell THE?

These days, some are quite sensitive to how our words and actions affect others. Perhaps to some, changing a few "he" words may feel like an insult. However, English has plenty of "he" words, so giving us this one shouldn't be a problem.

Besides, English isn't a protected class, and we've merely neutralized one word, which doesn't make it a word for us but removes it from the list of "he" words.

45

Use "the" or "tha" and voila! Can you <u>hear</u> that rusted, antique word scale moving up to neutralize English? Congratulations! It's about time! WEnglish for WEquality is making a difference! We don't want to make it harder for people to spell English words, but consider this: English has been treating a/an as two different words for *centuries,* so switching to "the" or "tha" should be a reasonable change. It's a common word, and it neutralizes English. All. By. Itself.

Note: We'll be asking dictionaries to change their primary spelling of "the" to "tha" and put "the" in parentheses as an alternative spelling. Dictionaries are impressed by the number of requests for word changes, and this is tha most important one. We can't wait to celebrate! But you don't have to wait for an official dictionary change. You can start using "tha" right away!

Change a Word, Share a Smile

> *"Any new idea is first ridiculed. Then violently opposed. Then accepted as self-evident fact."*
> —*Arthur Schopenhauer*[42]

Some people are downright offended as if we're committing some sinful or "wrongful" act by spelling an English word differently. Arthur Schopenhauer's quote above shows that when we instigate change, others need time to catch up. We hope you're getting prepared for a whole new *world.* Have you heard of quantum computers? Artificial intelligence? Changing tha spelling of a word in English is nothing compared to what the future holds for us as these new technologies unfold.

We'll see how dictionaries respond to our spelling suggestion. If they're on tha track of equality, they'll be inclined to support and change tha

---

[42] Our favorite pessimist is back with great insight on the process of introducing new ideas. https://quotefancy.com/arthur-schopenhauer-quotes

primary spelling of "the" to "tha." Change is always a cha(lle)nge. You're welcome.

<u>One more easy fix for "the."</u> Did you know that "the" is often an unnecessary word? We use it like bubble gum, duct tape, and wood filler. If we sense a word is missing in a sentence, we often fill it with "the" because it feels better.

But here's another excellent challenge to make English a better language: treat "the/tha" as if it's a taboo word and leave it out more often. We use it too much, killing great writing. In fact, "The" is considered a "dead" word by the authors of *The Bestseller Code*.[43]

Try this: As you're writing, if you feel the need to use "the," leave it out and check if you can do without it. Is there a more interesting way to write that sentence?

Try it here if you'd like to experiment.

Example: The truth is that we don't need the word "the" as much as we think we do (17 words).

How many words did you reduce it to? We cut it down to "We don't need 'the' so much."

Don't We Need to Change at Least Half tha "He" Words in English to Make It Equal?

Not at all. By changing a few of tha most common words, our goal is accomplished. Anyone can contribute to balancing English, but it's only necessary if they genuinely desire to do so.

---

43 Jodie Archer, Matthew Jockers, *The Bestseller Code* (2016), pp. 118–119 https://www.amazon.com/Bestseller-Code-Anatomy-Blockbuster-Novel/dp/1250088275

When I first worked with "the," I tried not to use it at all. Talk about frustrating! I realized what an impossible task that was. Suddenly, a new idea struck me, which solved that problem—using the English a/ an methodology. Always consider a different approach if something you're trying to do isn't working.

You'll notice that we leave plenty of "he" words untouched and don't try to change them. Why? Because it's our goal to *balance* English, not neuter it. Plus, taking on an entire language is an enormous job. It's essential to focus on what generates tha greatest impact with tha least amount of change.

Now that you've got the first word, use it and see what a difference it makes. Remember Anne Wondra's wise words: "I like easy."[44] We hope you agree. Finish this book, take note of these simple word changes, and let's get it done!

It's time to celebrate! The first word is done! English is neutralized!

---

[44] Phrase created by my book collaborator, Anne Wondra. I like it, don't you?

Chapter 9

Hell Yes, We Can Have (A Few) Words for Ourselves

We must do this, and it's so easy that you'll wonder why you didn't think of this before.

It's important that we *all* participate in this quest, but those of us who aren't men are wasting our own time—we're erasing ourselves unless we get serious about enhancing our equality, even with something as simple and powerful as words. My collaborator on this book and all my others, Anne Wondra, always says, "I like easy." Watch how even a one-word change can do that.

Remember—It's Not Just for Us...

Think about what becoming more invisible implies to those who fought valiantly for our right to be seen in their struggle for our right to vote. We must continue our ascent to equality because failure is not an option. Those who endured a century of tribulation to obtain those rights require us to do this, as well as our daughters, granddaughters, and all the women who will come after us. We can't afford to lose our ground.

It's time for us to make a conscious choice to neutralize English and equalize ourselves—to demand words that include us and then be brave enough to become equal. No more focusing on what others have or have not done to or for us or against us in the past. That era is over.

Our silence is not golden when it comes to English. In 1992 (a mere thirty-one years ago as I write this), linguist Robin Lakoff wrote, "As long as we are complicit in our voicelessness, there is no incentive, neither fear nor shame, to make anyone else change."[45] Such a powerful challenge by one of our own! We must do this!

The Merriam-Webster Dictionary defines voicelessness as "having no voice in the management or control of affairs. Powerlessness, impotence." How many of us feel that way?

Further, regarding the word "complicit," the dictionary states that "it literally means 'folded together.'"[46] This definition reminds me of folding the cake batter so that individual ingredients disappear. Is that what we want? That's harsh but also true. Are we simply going along with the flow rather than stirring up any issues—like changing a few words? Come on...we can do better!

Breaking the Words That Bind Us

"No dictionary of a living tongue can ever be perfect, since while it is hastening to publication, some words are budding and some falling away."—Samuel Johnson[47]

It's perfectly normal for a language to change its words. English adds several hundred every year.[48] So, let's introduce a few of our own without

---

[45] Robin Tolmach Lakoff, (1942) is a feminist and professor of linguistics at the University of California, Berkeley. Her writings have become the basis for much research on the subject of women's language.

[46] https://www.merriam-webster.com/words-at-play/a-brief-history-of-complicit

[47] https://www.goodreads.com/quotes/151271-who-will-consider-that-no-dictionary-of-a-living-tongue

[48] Each year, the lexicographers at the Oxford English Dictionary update the prestigious tome with new words. *In 2022, over 650 new words were added*, ranging from slang and tech terms to pop psychology words.

any "he" words attached. Are you ready to change tha spelling of a few more words in English to give five more words for our sex? We hope so because it's time to turn around and head back up the road to equality in English.

We've already changed one word. Now, how about a trip back to the 100 most common words in English?

Next Most Common Words

In numerical order, tha next most common "he" words in English are, at #11, he; at #18, his; at #19, they; at #23, this; at #37, when; and at #41, there. All of these words can be spelled differently to create words for us, but we want to focus on tha few that have a more direct link. Let's reclaim tha two "he" words for us in "The 100 Most Common Words Chart": #46, she, and #62, her.

Yes, "she" and "her" are the next most powerful and common words in English because these are the *first and only references* to those of us who aren't men in the 100 most common English words. What a tragedy! WFW believes that we should stop and pay particular attention to these words.

The etymology of "she" and "her": https://www.etymonline.com/ word/ she

Easy Fix #2 & 3: She to Shi and Her to Hir

She and her are both pronouns, and pronouns have been topics of hot debate in English for centuries (and still are). If you doubt it, pick up a copy of *What's Your Pronoun: Beyond He and She* by Dennis Baron.

He says, "There have always been so many ways to say something in English, and variation and change are natural, normal, and inevitable for any language. *Since all words are invented words* (emphasis added by the author), if you don't see a pronoun here that meets your needs, by all means, make one up." This statement terrifies but also consoles me since Baron is a Guggenheim Fellow and professor emeritus of English and linguistics at the University of Illinois. Just be aware of how confusing it can be to invent words that others might not understand. Therefore, good etiquette would suggest asking others what pronouns they use.

WFW spells her as "hir" and she as "shi" simply because we want to take "he" out of these words. "Er" and "ir" are both used in thousands of English words that are pronounced exactly tha same.

While we're obviously trying to ensure our changes make sense, it's not actually necessary. As Baron says, we can change a word's spelling just because we want to, but remember, we don't want to create chaos. Are you ready to spell some words differently to balance English?

Remember, WFW's goal is to give those of us who aren't men some of our own words, and we can't accomplish that if we allow these two highly common 'he' words to sneak in under tha bar. Fair is fair.

We hope you'll agree and try these. See how easy it is to give ourselves words?

When Does Any Word for Us Show Up?

"Man" is at word #16 on the 100 most common English words chart, but checking further, *there are no more words for us on the list!* Isn't that shocking? You'll find "woman" at #126, which is 110 words *after* "man." WFW doesn't take this lightly; we simply fix it.

Note: The 100 Most Common English Words list doesn't include plural words, which is why "men" and "women" don't show up. Disappointed? Try not to be. Imagine if all the plural words were included!

WFW doesn't suggest the complete removal or respelling of all the "he" words on the list; rather, the aim is to tip the English word scales into balance. If it bothers you that we're not tackling more, remember that our goal is to neutralize English (which we've already accomplished with "the/tha"). Now, we're making it more balanced by introducing some words of our own. By tha way, if you really want more word changes, we've got plenty identified in our WEnglish Glossary in tha "resources" tab at wenglishforwequality.com: https://www.wenglishforwequality. com/_files/ugd/5dbb58_322714f0d028487fba9c63bc7310036a.pdf

WFW seeks to balance English, not create chaos. If we change too much all at once, we may lead to language chaos, and no one wants that. Some of us may recall the biblical story of The Tower of Babel, where God induced chaos by confusing languages due to human arrogance. We don't want chaos; we want to understand each other because creative activity depends on our ability to share ideas. We aim to keep it as simple as possible. If we can universally agree to change these few words (even just one), we can accomplish our goal of making English a more equal language.

Recap

We have neutralized English in one word and given two alternative words for those of us who aren't men.

Change THE to THA
Change HER to HIR
Change SHE to SHI

So easy!

Woman & Women: Womun & Wimin

Now, let's turn our attention to the English words "woman" and "women." Can we make these words work without being "he" words? Yes, let's address them now.

Note: We're maintaining phonetic sounds while *spelling them differently (and in a more linguistically accurate manner).*

Etymology of woman/women: https://www.etymonline.com/word/women

Easy Fix #4: Spell It Like It Sounds!

Once again, we're turning to tha phonemic chart for insight (see Appendix 3).

These two words can be spelled better phonemically, as shown below. It's subtle but wise to take a gentle approach to a language that has not given us due respect. Observe how WFW linguistically spells these words.

Woman Becomes Womun

We seek words of our own. "Woman," as it's pronounced in English, is more linguistically correct when we spell it as "womun." There are several thousand words in English that use "un," and these words mirror the way most of us say "womun." This suits our purpose here.

"Un" can symbolize an "undoing," which is exactly what we want—we want to *undo* our ties to "he" words.

"Un" can also signify "not." We're *un*doing some "he" words to create words for ourselves. Therefore, womun can be defined as "not man" or "unman." It's sort of symbolic, isn't it? "Un" is also used in words like "unity" and the United Nations.

If you don't like the United Nations due to its predominantly male composition, then an objection to English seems justified. Note: Internationally, the UN actively supports what's called tha HeForShe movement (find out more at heforshe.org). If any international organization can break the bias of English, it would be a group that has such broad influence. You can view the 2023 conference highlights here: https://www.youtube.com/watch?v=RXp0F9LjAzY

Women Becomes Wimin

Spell it like it sounds—wimin.

What About "Female"?

This word is seldom used except with "male" or as a medical term, and it has derogatory connotations.[49] It does what all these other "he" words do—it links to a "he" word. WFW objects by not using it.

"Fe-<u>male</u>" wears a skirt and high heels to pretend it's a womun (if you're a guy who likes to do that, go ahead. We just want English to stop hiding its masculine power inside words for us). The etymology of "female" comes from tha Latin word, "femella" and is unrelated to "he" words (learn more at etymology.com).

---

[49] 1) "Female" refers to a sex of any species, while "woman" refers to human females; reducing women to their reproductive abilities is dehumanizing and excludes women who cannot reproduce, trans, and gender non-conforming people. It is not widely acceptable to refer to men as "males." "Female" is often used in a pejorative sense—*to insult or belittle.* See also 2)https:144//slate.com/human-interest/2014/08/using-female-as-a-noun-is-it-offensive-to-women.html#
3) of or denoting the sex that can bear offspring or produce eggs, distinguished biologically by the production of gametes (ova) that can be fertilized by male gametes. Definitions from Oxford Languages.

The power to decide what happens to words like this ultimately resides with you. You can choose words that honor wimin instead of ones that systemically weaken us.

My collaborator, Anne Wondra, observed that "fe" in "<u>fe</u>male" appears on the periodic table as a symbol for iron. Interesting, isn't it? Iron-male?

Additionally, "fe" also sounds like "fee," which further insults us. For these reasons and more, WFW doesn't use it. Are you wondering what we will do with "male" if we don't use "female"? Good question. We avoid using male, and that seems to work out well because "male" is easily confused with "mail." We prefer "man and womun" and "men and wimin" or our favorite word, "we." Besides, the terms male and female are also used to describe animals, which we are not.[50]

An Interesting Twist

In an interesting twist on a similar topic, *Unspinning The Spin* suggests reversing our tendency to put man titles *before* titles for us, thereby honoring us even more. Instead of "man and womun," try saying and writing "womun and man;" instead of "men and wimin," try "wimin and men." Or, what about Mrs. and Mr.? Wife and Husband? You'll find many such suggestions.[51]

Summary: We've neutralized tha most common English word and created four words of our own. It might not sound like much, but it's

---

[50] https://slate.com/human-interest/2014/08/using-female-as-a-noun-is-it-offensive-to-women.html

[51] *Unspinning The Spin*, p.185

good enough because we've worked on some of tha most common English words that affect us. These words don't sound any different, so it's an easy way to make English more balanced without confusing anyone with new pronunciations.

Remember Amanda Montell's words, "We're in a perfect position for a language revolution. We have the tools; we have the emotional insight." So let's do it! Our revolution requires no weapons, just some changes in word spelling. Are we willing to "break tha spell" of English so that we can have some words of our own? Isn't it about time?

Chapter 10

Tha Sixth Word

Three of the words we changed are pronouns. Did you know that over 100 pronouns exist in English, categorized into seven types?[52] We previously dealt we "shi" and "her," and now, we shall look at one more common pronoun

But first, what's tha purpose of pronouns anyway?

Personal Pronouns

A personal pronoun is *a concise and simple substitute for an individual's proper name.*[53]

"I," "you," "he," "she," "it," "we," "they," "me," "him," "her," "us," and "them" are *personal pronouns*, which means they can replace a person's name. Plenty more pronouns are not classified as personal pronouns.

---

[52] There are seven types of pronouns that both English and English as a second language writers must recognize: the personal pronoun, the demonstrative pronoun, the interrogative pronoun, the relative pronoun, the indefinite pronoun, the reflexive pronoun, and the intensive pronoun—Grammerly.com

[53] The main function of pronouns is to replace nouns. Because of this, they are used like nouns in sentences. Similar to nouns, pronouns commonly serve as the subject of a sentence, followed by a verb (a word expressing an action). —Scriber.com

We won't discuss each one in detail; however, a word of caution is essential—if we're lazy or unaware here, we could get lost. Examine tha list of personal pronouns. Do you see any "he" words? Certainly! Now, add "t<u>he</u>y," "t<u>he</u>ir," and "t<u>he</u>m" to our "he" word list. My, oh my!

They, Them, Their

Individuals who prefer not to conform to the gender binary (and we honor that decision) have embraced "they," "them," and "their" as gender-inclusive words.[54] Tha pronoun door is wide open with options, and that's perfectly acceptable. However, it can lead to confusion, as some of these chosen words can contradict our WFW efforts toward linguistic equality.

As far as WFW is concerned, all three of the above words are "he" words, and tha *last thing* English needs is more of those. Once again, tha masculinity of English hides in plain sight.

Is There a Solution for Pronoun Woes?

WFW wishes for an easy fix for these pronouns, but we must leave that to others more deeply involved in this arena, with one exception— the word "they," which is widely used in singular form. Even Dennis Baron, author of *What's Your Pronoun: Beyond He and She*, agrees that "they" is our best option because we're already comfortable with it and English has been searching for a better word for over a century! His entire fifth chapter is devoted to explaining why the singular "they" works.[55] It's been in use far longer than most of us have been alive.[56] Isn't it time to cease this word war?

---

[54] The concept of gender neutrality has been around for many years. It was first used in the academic context by philosopher *Michel Foucault* in his 1976 book *The History of Sexuality*. Oct 23, 2022

[55] *What's Your Pronoun: Beyond He and She*, pg. 149

[56] Ibid., since 1375 in the Old English romance known as "William and the Werewolf".

Easy Fix #6: They to Thay

The Oxford English Dictionary traces the singular "they" back to 1375.[57] We won't dispute that. In fact, we agree to the extent that it's the easiest way to solve a long-standing pronoun problem. Can we collectively agree to use it and stop trying to come up with better ideas? Centuries have passed, and too much time has been spent on one English word. Enough, agreed? Except for one minor spelling change, of course.

Instead of spelling it as "they," WFW spells it as "thay." That makes more sense to those of us who want fewer "he" words in English.

What About We, Us, Our?

How long have we grappled with pronoun choices? Can we all now accept a few word changes, recognizing that wimin deserve to be (indeed, are) equal to men, even if it's not fully realized in our reality yet? Men and wimin are more alike than other beings on our planet are to us.[58] Let's work with words that can draw us closer rather than drive us apart. That's our purpose in this pronoun section of BTBOE.

An Exercise With We, Us, Our

What about using we, us, and our to replace some pronouns? Since we're already expressing our pronoun preferences, let's include these. However, a challenge arises—we can't because it leaves us uncertain about who's included. Who is "we"? Who is "us"? Who is "our"? WFW loves what these words suggest in English. See below.

---

[57] Ibid.

[58] https://www.sciencedaily.com/releases/2021/03, *Massive Study Reveals Few Differences Between Men's and Women's Brains*, March 29, 2021

We

English has only a few "we" words, with Scrabble.com suggesting there are just over 1,000. And yet, there are some great "we" words to consider: "We" itself is wonderful and one of my personal favorites as in WEnglish for WEquality. It draws us together rather than separating us from others like "they," "them," and "their" do.

Wealth

WEalth is a favorite word for those that aspire to it (and its sole syllable is split into WE AL [TH], which is nice).

Well

"We-ll" is, well, a favorite because being "well" beats not being well.

Awe

And then, there's "a-we." What a word! It just might be the best word in English!

Us/Ous:

Another great word sound that's spelled in two different ways! What a different world we would live in if we cared more about each other. "Us" and "ous" are common spellings. Check any word-oriented website to find how many "us/ous" words we have in English. Let's use more of these more often. Yes, there are some "us/ous" words we don't prefer, but there are plenty that we do.

Exercise: What *uplifting* words ending in "us/ous" can you list without looking anywhere? Try these here:

A_____ B_____ C_____ D_____

E_____ F_____ G_____ H_____

I_____ J_____ K_____ L_____

M_____ N_____ O_____ P_____

Q_____ R_____ S_____ T_____

U_____ V_____ W_____ X_____

Y_____ Z_____

You probably listed more than one word per letter of the alphabet, didn't you? Yes, English can be fun! Using better words has the potential to uplift us and our world!

Another "us" word that people around tha word love is "Jesus." Not everyone, of course, but he has many followers. Could it be because it's an "us" word and Jesus was a loving example who still draws people, even over 2000 years later? That's how my mind works, so I wonder, and I like it.

Our

The Free Dictionary by Farlex lists 2228 "our" words in English. There are many great "our" words, including one that initially surprised me. Consider this, "our" is included in "your." Makes you think, doesn't it?

Yes, we like to separate ourselves from other's problems by saying, "That's *your* problem," sort of like Pontius Pilate did with Jesus when he washed his hands in front of tha agitated crowd that wanted to crucify him.

The connection between "our" and "your" made me stop and think. When I tell someone "That's your problem," am I really making sure they own that issue or could I subliminally (without realizing it, of course) be wrapping myself in with them? If "our" is a part of "your," it raises this question. As I've said, I'm not in a position to make any claims to psychological interpretations in English, but you have to admit that it's an interesting language that could be affecting us subconsciously.

Words don't belong to anyone. While trademarks are useful to protect works created from words, you can't own words. Email addresses that are already in use by others can be held privately and then sold, but you can't open a dictionary to a specific word and call it "my word" to prevent others from using it.

What you choose to do with my word ideas is up to you, and I can't force the world to accept what I think is an important concept. Here's my point—you can generally use whatever words you prefer. If you don't like tha words I have carefully chosen to change in this book, you're free to do whatever you want to with them. You can even decide to spell the words differently.

Wouldn't it be wonderful if a group of us could gather around these words and consistently use them to study their impact? As I said at tha beginning of this book, this is my personal thesis. I'm sharing because I'm eager to know if you think what I've discovered and written about is important. You don't have to do anything about it; it's your choice. But I do hope you'll consider what I've said here and apply it to your language skills as is comfortable for you—even if it's initially uncomfortable.

Chapter 11

Power Words

"The word is not just a sound or a written symbol. The word is a force; it is the power you have to express and communicate, to think, and thereby to create the events in your life. You can speak... The word is the most powerful tool you have as a human; it is the tool of magic. But like a sword with two edges, your word can create the most beautiful dream, or your word can destroy everything around you. One edge is the misuse of the word, which creates a living hell. The other edge is the impeccability of the word, which will only create beauty, love, and heaven on earth. Depending upon how it is used, the word can set you free, or it can enslave you even more than you know. All the magic you possess is based on your word. Your word is pure magic, and misuse of your word is black magic."
—Miguel Ruiz, *The Four Agreements: A Practical Guide to Personal Freedom*

"Words can destroy. What we call each other ultimately becomes what we think of each other, and it matters."
—Jeanne Kirkpatrick [59]

Science has long recognized that everything is composed of energy vibrating at different speeds and creating different outcomes based on

---

[59] https://quotefancy.com/quote/1275547/Jeane-Kirkpatrick-Words-can-destroy-What-we-call-each-other-ultimately-becomes-what-we

our focus.[60] If that's tha case, wouldn't it make sense to attend to words that activate our highest and best vibrations and, conversely, know which words pull us down into a more negative world?

WFW has created a short, alphabetical list of what we consider some of tha most uplifting words in English, as well as, au contraire, those that pull us down. We're including some of these here so that you can become aware and use word power appropriately. It could make a huge difference in your life experiences (numerous books focus on words for just that purpose).

Choose from our list below or make up your own; just be sure to add more wonderful words to your everyday speaking and writing and leave negative, nasty words behind as much as possible. As Amanda Montell shows so well in her book, *Wordslut*, there are far more nasty words for us than for men.[61] She asks, "Why, exactly, are there so many outrageous insults for women in the English language?" Why, indeed?

WFW List of High Vibration Words

A: All, Am, Amazing, And, Awe, Awesome
(Question: Why is "awesome" a good word and "awful" a negative one?)
B: Be, Because, Become, Believe, Best, Bliss, Brilliant C: Celebrate, Clarity, Create, Cure
D: Dear, Delight, Divine
E: Easy, Energy, Equal, Eternal, Every, Expand, Extraordinary

---

60 Rudyard Kipling poignantly declared, "Words are, of course, the most powerful drug used by [human]kind." This zealous statement was made during a speech Kipling gave in London in 1923, where he went on to describe how language enters into and influences "the minutest cells of the brain," a concept he could only deduce through his own observations of people and the world. Almost a century later, this reverence for the supreme influence of words is upheld across diverse modalities, from science to spirituality to the arts.

61 Amanda Montell, *Wordslut*, p. 23.

(Question: Why is extraordinary a positive word? Who wants to be "extra" of that?)

F: Fair, Fantastic, Fun, Funds, Free

G: Give, Glory(ous), Grace, Gratitude, Great, Grow

H: Happy, Heal (even though it's a "he" word that WFW doesn't prefer)

I: Idea, In, In–, –ing ("ing" can change a "shun" word usually spelled with a "tion" or "sion" ending into present progressive, which is much more powerful.

J: Joy

K: Kind, Know

L: Life, Love ("live" is excluded because spelling it backward is 'evil'.)
M: Magical, Magnify, Miraculous, More,

N: Now, Nurture

O: Open, Our, Outstanding

P: Passion, Peace, Power, Pro–, Prosperous, Purpose Q: Quality, Quest, Quiet

R: Radiant, Receive, Release

S: Sacred, Serene, Share, Shine, Soul, Sparkle, Spirit, Sure T: Thank, Thank You, Thrive, Transform, True, Trust, Truth U: Unique, Unite, Unity, Uplift, Us

V: Valid, Very, Victory

W: We, Whole, Wise, Wisdom, Wonder, World X: Hmm...

Y: Yes, Your

Z: Zealous, Zest

WFW List of Lowest Vibration Words

A: Alone, Anger, Ashamed, Asshole, Awful (it's interesting that "awe<u>some</u>" is such an uplifting word!)

B: Bad, Betray, Bitch, Blame, Boring, Bully, But

C: Cancer (WFW spells it "cansir," which makes it a "he" word), Can't, Compete, Cruel, Cunt

D. Damn, De–, Despair, Dick, Die–, Disease

E. Evil, Ex–

F. Fat, Fear, Foreign, Fuck

G. Garish, Grotesque, Guilt

H: Harsh, Hate, Helpless, Hurt I: Ick, Ill, –Ill, Insult

J: Judge K: Kill

L: Lack, Limit, Loser, Lost

M: Mis–, Miserable, Miserly, Misogyny N: Need, Never, No, Not, Nothing

O: Obese, Only, Overtly P: Pain, Poor, Pussy

Q: Quit

R: Race, Rage, Rape, Regret

S: Scared, Sexist, Shit, Shun, Sick, Sissy, Slut, Stupid, Sick, Sin, Sorry

T: Tease, Terrify, Terminal, Time

U: Use

V: Victim, Violate, Violent, Virus, W: War, Whore, Woe, Won't, Wrong

X: Execute

Y: Yellow

Z: Zero, Zilch

Chapter 12

And Etc.

"Communication produces the legs for bias, carrying it from person to person, from generation to generation. Eventually, however, communication will be the way to end discrimination."
—*Without Bias: A Guide for Nondiscriminatory Communication.*[62]

Dictionaries

Are you suggesting that we should spell words however we want to? Then what authority do dictionaries possess?

Let's be clear: dictionaries are our most authoritative references for words, their spelling, their meaning, their assigned role in English, and in some cases, their etymology. But words are a moving target, coming and going without notice.

We've kept our word changes to a minimum because we, like you, want to control rather than create chaos. At tha same time, you really can spell words however you want to. Just remember that other people should be able to understand us because our ability to communicate is key to our lives. Imagine not being able to understand each other!

---

[62] Judy E. Pickens, Without Bias, John Wiley & Sons, 1982

A Word About "You Guys"

> *"Calling women 'guys' makes us invisible. It says that 'man'—as a male—is still the measure of all things."*
> —Audrey Bilger[63]

I think that quote speaks for itself, but it's a hard habit to break. Some, like Amanda Montell, suggest "you all" instead of "you guys," which, she says (and we agree), is a bit Southern sounding, but it's a lot better than calling ourselves "guys." When I talk to groups, I tend to say, "Okay, everyone." "Friends" is also a nice touch.

What do *you* do to stop using "you guys" when referring to wimin?

What About Proper Names and Titles?

WFW honors all proper names and titles as they appear in English and does not suggest altering them through our work.

Did you know that "n-a-m-e" is a double "he" word because it can spell both "man" and "men"? You might not think much of it, but I spent a long time trying to come up with a different way to say the word. "What's your title?" or "What (or how) do you call (refer to) yourself?" all sounded awkward, and I figured I'd spend too much time explaining my intent. If you've got an idea, you know how to contact me.

I also discovered that, as I tried to remove proper names, English collapsed. Really. Shocking, isn't it? That's another sign that English depends on "he" words for its basic structure.

Consider how many men's names we use to refer to other objects in English. Here are a few examples:

---

[63] Audry Bilger is the current president of Reed College, and she previously served as the vice president and dean of Pomona College. She is the author of *Laughing Feminism*. Find her at presidentsoffice@reed.edu.

1) Al (very common ending to words—as in "evangelical.")
2) Bill (as in, "I'll need to bill you for this.")
3) Cooper (as in, "Let's try to cooperate.")
4) Dick (does anyone really need an example here?)
5) Ed (try forming a past-tense word without "ed"!)
6) Frank ("Frankly, my dear" or "May I be frank?")
7) Jim ("I think I'll go to the gym." Remember, WFW evaluates both spelling and sounds.)
8) Matt (as in, "What's tha matter" or "As a matter of fact." Even more critical, our words "matter" because quantum physics teaches that what we say can materialize.) *"Watch your thoughts, they become your words; watch your words, they become your actions; watch your actions, they become your habits; watch your habits, they become your character; watch your character, it becomes your destiny."*—Credited to both Lao Tzu and Gandhi
9) Ned (as used in the past tense: "I opened my mail and found a bill from tha gym.")
10) Paul (as in, "I find it appalling that wimin are treated so poorly.")
11) Stan (as in, "Stand up, please.")
11) Tim (as in, "I'm not that timid" or "I am not a 'victim.")
12) Van (as in "Should we take tha car or rent a van?")
13) Wes (as in, "I'm heading west for a vacation.")

And that's only a short list. However, WFW decided not to change these words.

Similarly, we did not alter book and song titles and all titles in general. Most of these are copyrighted, and if something already exists in English and belongs to someone else who created it, we want to honor that person. It's not our place to change it.

What About Using WFW at School or Work?

If you're in school or working in a setting in which you are obligated to spell according to the current English rules, do so. Ah, but during your quiet, private times and personal writing, spell these words your way and relish the satisfaction of knowing *you've created words that don't attach you to men.* Isn't it delic<u>iou</u>s? If doing that makes you uncomfortable, even in your personal space, please don't feel pressured. Now that you know these ideas, you can express them whenever you're ready.

Also, please remember to consult *Unspinning The Spin,* which contains hundreds of words that are equalized. Currently, it's our best resource for word substitutes. While it doesn't achieve what WFW does with tha six words we've changed, it has a wider focus and a much larger context.

Whether you're a womun or a man, your writing can show that you're in favor of equality by changing how you spell these six words and revising anything you're writing if you come across a "he" word. If anyone suggests your spelling is inappropriate, smile, say "Absolutely," and explain what you're doing and why—express your pride in it. Just don't ruin your career over it.

Remember, Most People Don't Understand…Yet

> *"The most difficult thing is the decision to act; the rest is merely tenacity. The fears are paper tigers. You can do anything you decide to do."*
>
> —Amelia Earhart[64]

> *"Progress is impossible without change, and those who cannot change their minds cannot change anything."*
>
> —George Bernard Shaw[65]

---

[64] https://www.ameliaearheart.com

[65] https://www.google.com/search?q=george+bernard+shaw+quotes+about+change&oq=-George+Bernard+Shaw+quotes+about+change&gs

"The world as we have created it is a process of our thinking. It cannot be changed without changing our thinking."

—Albert Einstein[66]

I believe that most people simply don't yet understand these "he" word codes that are obvious to those of us who know. Be kind and remember that many resist change, making these simple word spelling changes challenging. I've worked hard over the years to make what I've learned a gift to share easily, in a kind, gentle, and simple manner. I hope I've succeeded.

---

[66] https://www.bing.com/search?q=the+world+as+we+have+created+it+quo
te

Chapter 13

Unity or Uniformity?

"Unity, not uniformity, must be our aim. We attain unity only through variety. Differences must be integrated, not annihilated or ignored. Fear of difference is fear of life itself."

—Mary Parker Follett[67]

I hope you enjoy the few new words that finally give wimin words of our own in English! Let's use and share these spelling changes now— tha, shi, hir, womun, wimin, and thay. *We don't have to wait for dictionaries, although WFW is already at work on that.* Let's all simply enjoy using some words that respect us (remember, by birth or preference) and be happy about that.

Acting On Our Own Behalf

This also reminds us that whenever we come across a "he" word, it's up to each of us to decide whether to use it. It's that easy.

---

[67] https://seapointcenter.com/15-quotes-by-mary-parker-follett/#

Examples to have fun with:

1) U.S. <u>his</u>tory books tell us that the Fourth of July 1776 was the birthday of our nation.
REWRITE: _____

2) I'd like to think you can <u>man</u>age without me.
REWRITE: _____

3) I hope your broken arm is <u>heal</u>ing well.
REWRITE: _____

4) <u>Cer</u>tain people don't like modern music.
REWRITE: _____

5) Can you recom<u>men</u>d a good real estate a<u>gent</u>?
REWRITE: _____

6) I could use some <u>gui</u>dance here.
REWRITE: _____

My Mother's Business

Watching my mother suffer through life, hindered by the constraints of being a fundamental Christian, taught me that I could not repeat hir experience. I've learned to embrace who I am and to do what comes to me because that's how I want to live—boldly and fully myself. I want to be remembered for sharing my ideas, not hiding because I don't want to be shamed publicly like my mother was. Hir religion didn't appreciate hir lack of submissiveness, but shi taught me well.

It dawned on me the other day that *I'm completing my mother's unfinished business!* If shi had the freedom to do what shi wanted with hir life, I believe shi would have taken tha path I'm on or something similar. Shi was vibrant and powerful; yes, perhaps a bit too forceful in expressing what shi believed. But shi was honest, especially when speaking to a group. Another stroke of insight helped me realize that in my life's work, I'm continuing hirs in a gentle, easy way. If there's a next life—like I believe there is—if I ever see my mother again, I want to hear, "Well done, daughter!" I'm hoping my father will be by hir side and give me one of his famous bone-crushing hugs.

I've learned to approach others with care and respect rather than try to force my opinion on anyone—to plant a seed and move on. We each come to life with our own way of learning, unique challenges, gifts, and insights, which show tha world our individual preferences. These discoveries should be fun! When others attempt to sell us their ideas, a lot of us shy away, don't we? I'm offering what I've learned; that's my role. Share. Move on. Keep progressing because that's how life works. Step. By. Step.

Tha Crux of Tha Challenge

My work to make English a "we" language is important because we're moving toward a "we" world. Perhaps we're already there. Granting ourselves words is critical to our future. Let's take these small steps to make our "word world" more balanced and inclusive, to make us all more equal, and to respect and honor each other's uniqueness.

Did you know that six matriarchal societies still exist in our world?[68] In their book, *Half The Sky: Turning Oppression Into Opportunities Worldwide*, Nicholas D. Kristof and Sheryl WuDunn tell us the potential of our world.

"When women command greater power, child health and nutrition improve. A year after the Nineteenth Amendment gave women all across the country the right to vote in 1920, Congress passed the Sheppard-

---

[68] World Atlas https://worldatlas.com/articles/matriarchal-societies-around-the-world.html.

Towner Act, a landmark program for public health. The 'principal force moving Congress was fear of being punished at the polls' by the new women voters, one historian wrote. The improvement in America's health during this period was stunning...."[69]

When we empower ourselves and each other, good changes come about. However, our challenge remains that English needs to give us words, and we need to use those words to amplify our power. There's notable progress, but so much work remains. I hope my work with English paves the way in far less than three hundred years.

What could equality achieve for us that would make our world a better place for all to live in and share? We must remove obstacles that stand in our way, and I believe English is one such barrier. Let's give ourselves words and open the door to equality.

If we can change a few words and place more wimin in leadership, we might accomplish world peace (in less than three hundred years),[70] and if not world peace, at least word peace.

One Last WEnglish for WEquality Word

As I conclude this book, I'd like to share one word that sums up my work:

EVOLVE
which WFW converts to WEVOLVE

Why do I love this word? If you've followed how I learned to break words apart, mix up their letters, and find their core, you already know that WFW loves "we" words. In WEvolve, "love" can be spelled twice!

---

[69] Nicholas Kristof, Sheryl WuDunn, *Half the Sky, Turning Oppression Into Opportunity For Women Worldwide* (2009), Vintage Books, pp. 197–198

[70] Ibid., Footnote #10

(Remember, it's acceptable to use a second "O" according to the WFW word rules.)

Love times two. "Evolve" is defined by one dictionary as "to develop gradually, or to make someone or something change and develop gradually."[71] By channeling our sense of inequality into loving cooperation with each other, we can change our world. Step by step. Day by day.

Event by event. We can show our world a new way. Let's embrace our power to lead by love.

In hir heart-rending tale of finding love and then losing it in the death of hir beloved, neuroscientist Stephanie Cacioppo, a seasoned researcher of brain science, explains what love is and where it lives—in our brains, not our hearts.72 "Building healthy relationships," she says, "also builds a healthier brain, one that…can stave off cognitive decline, spur creativity and speed up our thinking. And there is perhaps no more powerful social activity, no better way of realizing our brain's full cognitive potential, than by being in love."

---

[71] https://dictionary.cambridge.org/us/dictionary/english/evolve

Epilogue

The Key to Equality Is Love

"Ending Patriarchy is one step in the direction of love."
—John Bradshaw[72]

Does that surprise you? The words of tha song that's playing as I begin this final section say, "Love is the message".[73] Honoring all of us with words is an act of love.

What I Now Know

I have grown through my work with words—from staunchly opposing equality for women to radically championing our pursuit of true equality. Amazing, isn't it, how that one word, "he," started my adventure?

And yet, perhaps it started when I was a young child, wearing my Sunday best to church, learning that Satan tricked Eve, leading us all into sin. This notion puzzled and then angered me. Why was it *our* fault—tha fault of women? Eventually, I decided it was a good thing Eve did what shi did because otherwise, we would all still be living without knowing tha difference between good and evil. I don't know about you, but I'd rather know than live in what some might consider blissful ignorance.

---

[72] John Bradshaw, *Creating Love: The Next Great Stage of Growth* (1992)

[73] https://en.wikipedia.org/wiki/Love_Is_the_Message_(MFSB_song)

I had to let go of a lot of outdated notions about tha subservient role of wimin because thay no longer made sense to me. Coming into my own power took time and courage but has been worth tha journey.

People ask me what I now believe in, almost two decades later, and I'm thrilled to declare tha following.

I Believe

As science (particularly quantum physics) now supports, there exists an intelligent, loving energy that manifests through us according to what we focus on (I like that there is an "us" in focus.) Yes, we are co-creators with Life, and we are given choices about what to do with that power (regardless of what we call it and whether we believe in it). In that way, Life carries on its great work through us, according to what we decide. Mere mortals sometimes think they can define this energy and give it a male identity. We have a nasty habit of separating ourselves from each other and love into hair-splitting ideologies despite originating from this same Source of Life. Ridiculous!

Now, let's collectively look at our larger world and ask: *Do we like what we're creating?* Yes? No? Some of it? Then, as we've done throughout this book, let's ask tha next question: *How can we fix what we no longer prefer? How can we make our world greater for all of us?*

I started this book with a quote by Arthur Schopenhauer: *"Thus, the task is not to see what no one has yet seen but to think what nobody yet has thought about that which everybody sees."*—Arthur Schopenhauer, *Notable Pessimist*

You now possess a deeper knowledge of English words than before we started this journey. You know how to decide whether a word is suitable for use or best avoided. You know how to transform "he" words by changing how they're spelled or selecting a different word altogether.

My work is complete for now. I hope it has influenced your perspectives so that you see English differently and choose to use these words and tools to make it a language that works for all of us. Even changing one word to neutralize English can make a huge impact! WEnglish for WEquality.

Thank you!

Acknowledging Others

I recall a time when I inadvertently omitted someone's name from my list of acknowledgments in a book I had written, and it was disastrous. I still don't know if I've been forgiven, but I had to learn to forgive myself.

After working on WEnglish for WEquality for so long, I hope I will be excused if I accidentally exclude or overlook someone. After all, I'm seventy, and although I don't believe age makes a difference when it comes to remembering facts, I admit that some "stick" better than others. Chronologically, as best I can, for this book, I thank...

My parents, Sterling and Wanita Mae Theobald, gave me life and understood my desire to write. They enrolled me in a writing correspondence school when I was sixteen because that was the only option back then to learn to write beyond the high school level. Both of them have passed into a new life through what we erringly call "death."

My older sister, Cheryl Ann (Theobald) Cook, left this world far too soon but not without gifting me with a story idea that became the award-winning novel, *Death by Roses*.

My brother, Paul Theobald, has faithfully supported my writing process. He's also one of the greatest "punners" I know, although he and I compete occasionally. He and his wife, Jodi, travel in their RV to wherever they're required by family and friends in times of crises, to solve engineering challenges for the company my brother often works for, and to serve God by showing love in every way they can.

My younger sister, Mary Hunter, who has long loved me, and I, her, even though we didn't talk to each other for several years (this sister stuff can get intense!). After a few years, Life brought us back together. We're now closer than ever. She's an amazing womun, who gets my writing life and reads my books long before others in my family. She's also a nurse, a massage therapist, and a womun with healing energy. She lives in the Rocky Mountains, where she hikes as often as she can.

My best friend on earth, Susie, whom I met during the delicious years between marriages when I was single and so unsure of myself. She knows all my deepest secrets and fears and remains my longest and truest friend.

My husband, Thomas Probst, has known me even longer than I've been writing and is still with me. That's saying a lot because, in case you don't know it, writers spend inordinate amounts of time alone doing their work. Tom doesn't read everything I write as soon as I write it, but he's a wonderful editor and a very wise, intelligent man. After thirty-seven years of marriage, we still laugh a lot and share tender moments. He gets me, and I adore him!

Anne Wondra, who I like to say is a "wond_ra_ful" person. We met over a decade ago when I was advertising for a travel partner during tha most intense years of my consulting career. She responded to my ad and has become so much more than a travel partner. Muse, friend, a womun of wisdom, and a wonder womun who taught me how to find my own wisdom. Anne has profoundly collaborated with all my published works. You can find Anne at www.wonder-spirit.com.

Rita Hale, whom I met through Anne. Rita is what I call a "medicine womun." She can travel through time and get to core issues when I'm stuck and unable to find my way alone. You can find Rita at haleritak@gmail.com.

Mikaela Jade Seely, who came to work for me during my consulting business years has assisted me with my writing work in myriad ways, mostly as a dazzling graphic artist, designing most of my book covers. Mikaela has found her way into tha gaming world, which she truly loves. I miss her.

Betty Neau, tha "wonder womun" who showed up to buy me out of my national consulting business so that I could devote myself to writing. She's now involved in the affordable housing world, as I was. There are very few company buyouts that work and even fewer that blossom into long-term friendships. I consider myself very blessed. You can find Betty at betty@theopro.com.

Lisa Anne, my astrologer, has been a consistent presence in my life. Those who underestimate the aligning of stars and planets are missing out on one of life's wonders. Lisa Anne and I have been working together for years, and while I was writing *Breaking The Bias of English*, we met every two weeks. You can find her at contacts@ pathwaysoflight.org. When I felt like I couldn't go on, she lifted me up. And for that, I'm grateful.

Michelle Lawrence, tha designer behind this wonderful book cover for *Breaking The Bias of English*. Thank goodness for people who understand the graphic world! Find her at m7awrence@icloud.com (I just noticed that "cloud" can also spell "could"!).

Mitch Mitchell, my hairstylist, whom I met after Tom and I moved to Doty Island in Neenah, WI, in 2021. Mitch is so much more than a hairstylist. His profound insights as we talk about my work and his joy in sharing with others inspire me constantly. Thank you, Mitch, for helping me "go grayer" with such ease!

Betsy Krizenesky, whose last name I still don't say correctly. Betsy became a neighbor when Tom and I moved to Doty Island. A brilliant and articulate womun, Betsy taught Russian at Lawrence University until she retired after tha spring term of 2022. She has also taught me so much about English. I especially thank her for introducing the concept of "neutralizing" English with "the/tha."

Sally Heidtke, an author I met at the end of 2022 during a book event she was hosting at Mitch's hair salon. I've never had a friend who writes, and Sally's work continues to influence mine. You can find Sally at sally.heidtke@gmail.com.

My Neighbors, Cate Wilson and her grandson, Aidan, provided instantaneous technical support at the end of this process.

I would call these people my "inner circle," and while there are many others who have shared in my journey with this book and supported my exploration of "WEnglish for WEquality" through it, this is my true tribe.

In tri-umph, Vivian Probst, 12/06/23

A Chat with Vivian Ruth Probst

Vivian, thank you for writing *Breaking The Bias of English*. It must have taken a lot of courage to step out into the world with these concepts. How did you handle the (tha) project for fifteen years without giving up?

What a fantastic lead question! Thank you. I would like everyone to know that I wrote through fear and self-ridicule almost every day. It was very hard, but the way I was introduced to this concept was so amazing that I couldn't stop just because I was scared. Lifework is like that; you do it anyway. It takes all the courage you have, faith, and some friends to encourage you. In my heart, I knew I had to complete it. Those who know me best are all thankful that it's done.

What was it like to leave the life you'd been raised to live, especially to change those beliefs?

That was very hard too. You must have faith in yourself and resolute belief in what you're doing. One of my key thoughts was that I wanted to speak for those who couldn't speak for themselves; I wanted to give us words that could change our male-dominated "word world" without creating a lot of chaos. I also wanted to do this for my mother because I am sure she would have enjoyed her life more if she'd been able to speak without being shushed.

Some readers are probably in that awful position right now. I hope my work encourages them. Take small steps, if you can. I had to confront an entire male council, who sent me, my husband, and our children back to the U.S. from Senegal, West Africa because I refused to submit to their teachings any longer. We had trained for over seven years, and we were home in six months.

It's also true that I developed an infection, very common among Africans at that time, but not among Americans. It gave me a physical reason to leave, but underneath was a more serious root cause that took much more time to recover from.

How have your beliefs changed in the past forty years since you left missionary work?

I love to share this! After I left, I spent several years out of touch with any sense of a divine being. I was angry because I felt like I had been led to a life that wasn't mine, and yes, I spent a lot of time b-laming others. That's where the Waukesha Women's Center (twcwaukesha.org) came in.

I've already recounted the absolute miracle it was to find that organization because it had only recently been created. As I whined about how I'd been raised, one of the counselors waived all that aside and said, "Okay. That's over. Let's focus on how you're going to live from now on." I needed to hear that because I wouldn't be where I am today if someone hadn't been blunt with me. It's not that I didn't need help to get from where I was; it was that the Women's Center's job was to get me to a position where I could take care of myself and my family. I needed a job—the rest would come later.

I left the religion I had been raised in, and yet, I never left my idea of a God who loved and cared for me (except as explained above). I had that to carry me through the tough times. Even my parents didn't know what to do with me. I eventually gave my former husband custody due to his relentless pursuit. This was back in the time when the custody of children was negotiable. He wasn't a bad man; he loved his children, and I had no idea where I was heading or what I would become. I believed the children were safer with him.

What's so incredible is that my parents came back to me after a few years. I had a great full-time job—I even looked very different—and they said, "Ruth (that was my name back then), we don't know why you had to go through what you did, but we like the changes we see in you." That made a big difference to me as I was welcomed back into the family, although we all knew that I saw things differently.

Here's the short version of what I believe in:

God is Love.

God does not send us to hell (because there is no hell—although, sometimes, this lifetime can feel that way).

God will always take care of us and love us, no matter what, but will not force us against our will. If we don't like how our lives are going, we have tha power to change that.

God is so much more than we can imagine. That's why I reject any sex or gender (especially the male version) given to that divine energy. Why do we keep trying to convince ourselves and others that we must believe a particular idea or God will reject us?

I detest denominational issues that divide people who love God but feel they must follow a particular teacher. Who are we to decide what God is or isn't? I like to consider "God" as a Divine Energy Source of love, and I love to share that energy with others.

Most of your writing is fiction, which you call "Intention Fiction." What is Intention Fiction and why did you write *Breaking The Bias of*

English, which is entirely non-fiction? Was it hard to change from one genre to the other?

My writing life started with a dream on March 10, 2000. My financial life was in chaos at that time. I was making a lot of money, but I kept spending it all. I finally asked myself what was causing that issue. That night, Book One of "The Avery Victoria Spencer Fables" *came to me in a dream.*

Intention Fiction is how I describe my novels because each one came to me while I was facing a particular issue (despair, weariness, rage, fear of death). I love that the story opens me up through "magical realism" so I can see, through my characters, the lessons I can learn.

Writing, for me, has always been like putting a puzzle together without knowing what the final picture will look like. I had always liked writing as a child, but this was different because each book was a story that made a real difference in my life. For instance, when Book One was finished, I was out of debt and decided to publish it myself. That book is now a part of a four-book series. I have also written two nonfiction works. One is my memoir, titled "I Was a Yo-Yo Wife…Until I Learned THIS!" *Now, there's* "Breaking the Bias of English" *as well.*

All of my writing comes to me from what I call 'Life'. I don't script anything; I simply write what I'm given by staying tuned to what I'm writing about and listening to my inner world. I've got almost thirty years of writing under my belt, so each book has taken me several years to complete.

For me, every life issue is a precious lesson, a gem I receive as I learn after going "inside" to fix the issue. I take a "story journey." <u>*I don't b-lame others for my issues; I first go inside and ask for my lesson.*</u> *For instance, I wrote* "I Was a Yo-Yo Wife…until I Learned THIS!" *when I learned why my second marriage wasn't working. I learned so much that I had to write about it.* "THIS," *mentioned in the book's title, refers to the "law of reflection," which immediately fixed my relationship with my husband. He had no idea that I was using him as a "test model" for what Life was teaching me, but the results were incredible and remain so to this day. We've been married thirty-seven years.*

"Breaking The Bias of English" also came to me as I was writing fiction. I'm a linguist by training, so words and language interest me greatly. When I became aware of how very masculine English is (even though we are all now so much more conscious of equality), I knew I had to write my way through to fixing that problem. What a fascinating journey it's been! I don't know what others will think of my work (that's true of everything I write), but I always know what I'm supposed to write about, and it comes to me as long as I stay open.

Final question for now: What's coming next? What should we expect to see from Vivian Probst?

First, a nice, long sabbatical. My husband deserves my time and attention. He's lived the past twenty-three years sharing me with my writing life, which has been like sharing me with a passionate lover, so to speak. Second, I've had so many books circling overhead for so long that I've always gone from one to tha next one in short order. It's time to hit the pause button.

What I really want to do is talk about what I've learned in my life and how it's all made such a difference—especially my work with English. I've been a national speaker for years, and I love it. If I can support others on their journey to waking up to their true life and work with wimin to foster equality, all my dreams will have come true.

Stay tuned. I didn't say I'm not going to write anymore. All I know for now is that I get to take a break, which I want to share with my family. I'm pretty sure they don't believe I can do it, but we'll all find out together.

Vivian R. Probst, 12/03/23.

Appendix 1

The "He" Word Chart

'HE' Words		'OUR' Words	
1	2	3	4
	# of English Words		# of English Words
He	8,270	She*	0
Man	2,148	Woman*	0
Men**	2.539	Women*	0
Him/Hym	238	Her*	0
His	2,039	Hers*	0
Male	183	Female*	0
Subtotal	**15,417**		**0**
Guy	203		
Sir	592		
Cer**	3,004		
Total	**19,216**		**0**

Appendix 2

The 100 Most Common Words in English

1. the	21. at	41. there	61. some	81. my
2. of	22. be	42. use	62. her	82. than
3. and	23. this	43. an	63. would	83. first
4. a	24. have	44. each	64. make	84. water
5. to	25. from	45. which	65. like	85. been
6. in	26. or	46. she	66. him	86. call
7. is	27. one	47. do	67. into	87. who
8. you	28. had	48. how	68. time	88. oil
9. that	29. by	49. their	69. has	89. its
10. it	30. word	50. if	70. look	90. now
11. he	31. but	51. will	71. two	91. find
12. was	32. not	52. up	72. more	92. long
13. for	33. what	53. other	73. write	93. down
14. on	34. all	54. about	74. go	94. day
15. are	35. were	55. out	75. see	95. did
16. as	36. we	56. many	76. number	96. get
17. with	37. when	57. then	77. no	97. come
18. his	38. your	58. them	78. way	98. made
19. they	39. can	59. these	79. could	99. may
20. I	40. said	60. so	80. people	100. part

Appendix 3

Phonemic Chart

monophthongs				diphthongs		**Phonemic Chart** voiced unvoiced	
iː sheep	ɪ ship	ʊ good	uː shoot	ɪə here	eɪ wait		
e bed	ə teacher	ɜː bird	ɔː door	ʊə tourist	ɔɪ boy	əʊ show	
æ cat	ʌ up	ɑː far	ɒ on	eə hair	aɪ my	aʊ cow	
p pea	b boat	t tea	d dog	tʃ cheese	dʒ June	k car	g go
f fly	v video	θ think	ð this	s see	z zoo	ʃ shall	ʒ television
m man	n now	ŋ sing	h hat	l love	r red	w wet	j yes

VOWELS / CONSONANTS

The 44 phonemes of Received Pronunciation based on the popular Adrian Underhill layout   adapted by EnglishClub.com

91

Appendix 4

Vivian's List of Subtle Abuses

The following list is for anyone who feels detached, blue, stuck, or can't help but see tha world and its events as consistently negative. Perhaps one of these subtle forms of being unloved—these orphans— is begging for love and attention. (Excepted from my book, *I Was A Yo-Yo Wife, Until I Learned THIS!*" I also like to title it, *How I Saved My Marriage in Ten Minutes [After Practicing "THIS" for Eight Years].)*

Vivian's list of subtle abuses:

1. Abuse of punishing: Being raised in an environment where you are scolded or punished even if you haven't done anything "wrong." Often, tha punisher is an adult taking their rage out on a child.

2. Abuse of disrespect/bullying: People constantly tell you that you're wrong, push you around, make fun of you, call you names, or hurt you because they're stronger and then say "I was just kidding" or "I didn't mean to hurt you (again). Stop being so sensitive."

3. Abuse of indifference: People close to you are too busy for you. "Children should be seen and not heard." "Leave me alone; can't you see I'm busy?" I'm not sure where parenting with both hands texting on a cell phone comes in. It also counts as being inattentive.

4. Abuse of superiority: People regularly remind you that they are older, wiser, and more talented than you (This is particularly aggravating when *that someone* acts like you have no idea what they are talking about when you do. We could all enjoy life much more if we treated each other as intelligent people and asked questions before making assumptions (still a sore spot for me at my age!).

5. Abuse of rejecting/disagreeing: People make it a habit to disagree with you no matter what and then combine it with #5.

6. Abuse of neglect: People who are supposed to look after your basic needs do not do so. Children are left to fend for themselves or placed in the care of abusive people.

7. Abuse of under-protecting: People regularly allow you to be exposed to dangerous or harmful situations without any form of protection.

8. Abuse of over-protecting: People are always around, telling you what to do and how to do it. You are fearful that something could go wrong. You are not allowed to have any time to explore the world around you on your own.

9. Abuse of expected performance: People regularly tell you what their expectations are and the consequences of not living up to them (such expectations are often unreasonable.)

10. Abuse of non-acceptance or non-forgiveness: People regularly make you feel responsible for things that go wrong and then refuse to forgive you. This is particularly harmful if you have done nothing wrong.

11. Abuse of self-absorption (aka narcissism): You only exist to make people feel good about themselves. People expect you to always praise them, often negating yourself in the process.

12. Abuse of religion (particularly if it diminishes wimin's freedom): You are regularly being told that because you are a womun, you are inferior to men; you are bad or sinful. You are threatened with hell so that you become fearful of a male god's ability to punish you eternally.

13. Abuse of positive thinking: People regularly tell you that you need to be happy regardless of how you feel inside. They do not allow you to cry or express angry feelings.

14. Abuse of language: This topic has been dealt with in *Breaking the Bias of English*.

15. Abuse of past lives: Sometimes, there is no other explanation for how you feel except that during a past life, you were subjected to something that caused you to bring negative feelings about yourself into this lifetime. Past-life regression therapy is amazing. I leave this discussion to the experts in that field.

16. Abuse of broken promises: Others regularly disappoint you by making promises and then not following through. Sometimes, there's a good reason, but if someone can't be trusted to do anything but disappoint, a form of abuse settles in, especially in early childhood. Worse yet, when someone goes back on a promise to you or takes it away as punishment when you had no idea that was a possibility.

Any of these sixteen topics could be greatly expanded. My purpose here is to raise awareness to help resolve them. Always seek professional support.

Appendix 5

Fabulous Five Focus™

(**S**ee below)

I created this brief document years ago, inspired by the power of thought and energetic vibrations in shaping outcomes. It's a fun tool to be used daily because it helps to decide on five things one would like to accomplish and then let go of until that evening. Before bedtime, it's amazing to look at that list and see what was accomplished on each item that day. Sometimes, you don't have to do anything because the matter gets cleared up or moves ahead as if by magic.

(There's also a place to ask for a "special surprise" and to list it when it occurs because we never know what Life has in store for us.) These sheets make it easy to remember everything there is to be grateful for (notice how WFW spells it).

Fabulous Five Focus™
(5 One-Minute Magical Moments)

Item #	✓	Description	Start 1-10	End 1-10
1				
2				
3				
4				
5		Surprise me with something WONDERFUL today!		

Signature _____   Date: _____

Having FUN with the Fabulous Five Focus

* Feeling Scale

1	I know it--I can see it!
2	Anything is possible!
3	I love the idea of it!
4	My hopes are up!
5	Wouldn't it be nice?
6	It wouldn't hurt to try.
7	I don't see a way.
8	It probably won't work.
9	I don't have time/money
10	It will never happen.

Progress Notes

Got a minute? That's all it takes to make your dreams come true!

Under **Description** above, identify up to **5** items you would like to see happen. Use the **Feeling Scale*** to identify how you feel right now about your ability to accomplish each. Enter that # in the **Start*** column.

Now, close your eyes. Focus on one item. Envision the _outcome you would like to see_ **FOR ONE MINUTE.** Your goal is to move up the Feeling Scale*, _even if it's just one step_. Feel it like you want it.

Open you eyes and in the **End** column write down the **Feeling Scale*** # you reached. Repeat process for each item. When finished, leave this page where you will see it at the end of the day.

Each night note any progress in the **Progress Notes**. Prepare to be uplifted!

Backstory

My upbringing prepared me for this book in ways I could not have imagined. Always a curious child, I loved to take on impossible projects because I wanted to contribute something meaningful to the world. At one point, I began rewriting the Bible so that children could understand it. I must have been eight or nine years old. I gave up once I got to the "begats" in Genesis. Glad I did!

As a child, I wrote musical numbers and created plays with my cousins. Unfortunately, by the time we had our "acts together," it would be time for my cousins to leave, so we never got to perform our creations. We begged and pleaded, but our parents, being busy, had no time for our "novel" ideas.

My mind has always thrived on creative challenges. The quest to gain understanding has always been my primary focus, and I believe I came by it naturally, as my father's family included four men and two women who went as missionaries to other countries and worked to translate the Bible. They were brilliant, God-fearing people.

My mother was also gifted in extraordinary ways, but the world into which she married put her in a subservient position. She became a doctor's wife and worked hard to follow the expectations of that role. It was hard for her to be left behind to raise four children while her husband, my father, met with patients, saved lives, and was loved because of his compassionate disposition.

Coming from an ev-an-gel-i-cal family with fun-da-men-tal beliefs (two fabulous word splits), I understood only one way of perceiving God—as a man. As a sinful woman, I needed to be saved. And so I was, truly, at the age of thirteen. All those years I was growing up, I felt begrudged for being a woman because we were, of course, the reason for sin in the world, which put us at the mercy of God and men. I recall thinking that it wasn't fair. It wasn't that I wanted to be a man; it was that I wanted to be considered equal to them. That thought never left me and has driven my work all these years later.

After letting go of the idea that I'm restricted by my genitalia, I've had a marvelous life. I became quite successful as a national trainer of complex housing regulations and traveled the country, sharing knowledge with anyone who would listen. It was an important housing program that began under the Reagan administration and still exists today. It continues to expand almost forty years later.

I was a student of the regulations I taught. I ensured I had a solid foundation so that I could get up in front of a group and give them a basis for any position I took. I loved teaching, and the adults in my classes appreciated my knowledge and style of presenting. Eventually, I even had my own company—something I had never dreamed of!

But my heart always ached for wimin. I had left my first marriage because I could not be submissive to my first husband. We had been in Africa at the time, and after I was counseled to change my ways (and couldn't), we were dismissed—excommunicated as it were—and it was my fault. But I couldn't go back. Once I realized that I had to tell the truth about what I believed instead of mouthing the words of others, I had to stop pretending, and that brought my husband, me, and our two children back to the U.S.

I still believe much of what I was taught, but I could not reconcile myself to be obedient to any man (including a husband) just because the Bible *inferred* it to be so. My mother had had the same challenge, so I decided it was time to let go of what I'd been taught and forge ahead. She had suffered terribly for hir inability to be an obedient wife, and I love hir bravery. When shi died at age sixty-five, I vowed that I would move her mission forward on behalf of all wimin. Little did I know where that would take me!

It's not like I was sure of myself. Dear God, no! I truly believed that my actions would displease God and that He would take my life, but I was desperate to find my own way. No more hiding.

During my divorce and custody battle in the early 1980s, I decided to allow my soon-to-be ex-husband to see if he could handle raising our children. He had been adamant about fighting for custody because of the change in me. I don't blame him—he no longer knew who I was, what I believed, or how I would raise our young children. He had a respectable job, so we decided that he could be the primary custodial parent.

I had no idea how that decision would affect my life. Not long after, he remarried, and I watched helplessly as my children were brought up by a different woman. While I have always felt the pain of not being able to raise my children, I have stayed close to them in the best way I can. They, of course, are now married with children.

I'll never have the privilege of raising them, but I try to accept that, and based on the circumstances as I understood them at the time, it seemed like the best option. I've learned to forgive myself and trust Life to heal our wounds.

Life took a different path when I began to live in the world of business, which I found myself well-suited for. The Women's Center in Waukesha, WI, saved me when I enrolled in their (then titled) "Displaced Homemakers' program." I could not have made this journey without them. I look back with great gratitude for how they supported me and my career.

I believe that as we age, we can look back and discern some magical and miraculous events that created our life journeys. There's no need to go into details here, but I always treasured my role as a woman and as a mother, so that guided my life. Regrets? Hell, yes! But mostly, I'm grateful for my wonderful life.

Because of my personal history and the trauma of the divorce, I grappled with anxiety, panic, and depression, which had always stomped on the women in our family. I had thought it was because of our religion, but once I was free of that structure, I still felt deep fear and considerable unworthiness. Therefore, I sought counseling. I wanted to be an encourager to other women.

The more I grew in my understanding of who I was and what I could do for others, the more I wanted to share it with everyone I encountered. Somehow, through all the twists and turns of my life, this guiding principle has remained steadfast. To this day, I remain strong in my resolve to help women grow into their true selves though we still have a long way to go to achieve equality.

I had no idea that working in the affordable housing industry would be my way into a perfect path: working with the housing needs of low-to moderate-income families (headed mostly by single-parent women), writing novels, and making English a better language for both men and those of us who aren't. My linguistic training from years ago has grown into my life's work.

In writing this book, I've had to learn to live through skepticism, not only of others but also my own as I explored English from a womun's perspective. I wasn't always sure it was a worthy undertaking because I spent a lot of time doubting myself and being highly critical. Nothing can enervate a body of research as quickly as a world that disagrees. I was so sure that no one would publish my work that I did it myself with Anne Wondra and others supporting me.

As I recalled all tha wimin before me who overcame tha bias in their work, I knew I had to finish. When you think of thoughts that others haven't thought of before, you must be prepared to stand strong on behalf of your own creative life.

Rededication

Written in WEnglish for WEquality

This book is dedicated to

Generations of wimin whose work has gone uncredited, whose discoveries are considered of merit, yet the wimin themselves remain invisible.

Wimin whose contributions were credited to men because thay were deemed inconsequential, even though thay worked tirelessly with little compensation.

Women who raised families and overcame obstacles behind tha scenes, enduring tha label of being considered "less than" by men while passionately engaging in brilliant work that went unseen.

To all these wimin who persevered through incredible obstacles, I owe great gratitude. Their courage laid the underpinnings of my life's work with words—

Driving me into the depths of our world's most common language to uncover the agony of a man's English and tha miracle of breaking that code so that we can all partake equally...

In a language that is neutralized with one word, giving wimin some words of our own and thereby balancing a "he" language into a "we" language as it should be!

Simple Tricks to Create a More Balanced English

With over 170,000 words in English, creating a way to give wimin more visibility among words might seem daunting. Here are some simple ideas that will pave tha way. Most of these are designed to reduce the number of "he" words in English.

1) Watch out for "he" words as explained in this book. Below, I'll show you a few more alternatives, although you can easily find these on your own using your computer search engine. Just don't drive yourself crazy.

2) Remember that "he" words not only include "he" but also "man," "men," "his," "him," "sir," and "guy."

3) Avoid "double 'he' words" that include more than one "he." Example: commandment. Can you feel tha power of that word?

4) "En": Turn your energy on with "in" words. Instead of words like "engage," try "ingage." Instead of "energy" try "innergy." Does that feel good?

5) "Eve" words can be derogatory: evil.

6) "Great": WFW likes to spell "grateful" as "greatful" to remind us that we are each on the earth to exude our greatness. My vehicle license plate says JSTBGR8!

7) "Heart"/"heal": Think about what these words are saying before you decide to use them.

8) Watch out for "her" words that are negative, such as "hurry up!" or "hurt." I changed my first name from Ruth when I realized that tha word "hurt" can be spelled with tha same letters. You don't have to do it, but for me, it was essential.

9) "His" words such as "history" can easily be replaced with actual dates, "the past," "long ago," "recently," etc. "This" is a word WFW allows.

10) "Hys–": Used for medical terms such as "hysteria" and "hysterectomy," derived from the Greek word "hystera," which means uterus. https://www.dailycardinal.com/article/2022/11/history-of-hysteria#:~:text=The%20Greek%20root%20word%20 hysteria,uterus%20roaming%20a%20woman's%20body

11) "IL–/–ILL": Illusion, illustration, Bill, dill, fill, hill, jill, kill, mill, nil, pill, quill, sill, still, til, will, etc.

12) "Man" words can be changed. For example, "human" can be replaced with "homo sapiens," "person/people."

13) "Mis–/Miss": The Free Dictionary by Farlex tells us that 1,925 words begin with "mis." If that bothers you, substitute them with a different word.

14) "Men" words can be changed. "A-men" can be substituted with "and so it is," "let it be so," or another favorite spiritual phrase.

15) "–ment" words can often be replaced with "ing," turning a "he" word into a present progressive activity. Achievement becomes "achieving," "government" becomes "governing," and so on.

16) Romance is another big "he" word.

17) Service is another potentially troubling word (sir-vice). It

sounds like a good thing to do—service to your country, service to others. You can decide if it's okay.

18) "Sh–" Words that tell us to be quiet or shush can be disquieting. "Sh-am-e" is a big one.

19) "Shun" words are those that end in "tion" or "sion," often pronounced with a "shun" sound. WFW prefers not to "shun," whether by spelling or pronunciation. We replace these words with "ing." See ("Men") above.

20) "Sir" words include those that sound like "sir," even if these are spelled with "cer" or other letters. Watch what comes up with our English word "cancer." It changes to "cansir," which begs the question: Is cancer a word that suggests submitting to someone or something, (as in "yes, I can, sir")? It's okay to submit under a lot of sircumstances. Just ensure that tha usage is not negative. Some websites suggest that sirtain cansirs are caused by anger.

21) "Sic/Sick": Need I say more?

22) "Sorry": If we say "thank you" instead of "I'm sorry," I believe our world would tip right side up.

23) "Terminal" splits into "term-in-al." Whether referring to an airport, corridor, or an illness, I'm not a fan for obvious reasons.

24) "Together" splits into "to-get-her." Don't use it if it makes you uncomfortable. WFW likes "togather" because it feels so good!

Thousands of ideas can show up as you work or play with English. Be sure to *injoy*, in joy!

The full chart is available at wenglishforwequality.com/copy-of-wen-glish

Left is Vivan Probst; right is Anne Wondra

www.ingramcontent.com/pod-product-compliance
Lightning Source LLC
Chambersburg PA
CBHW021119130626
46554CB00002B/770